"*WHEN YOU* find someone wh[o ...] better, you have found an incre[dible ...] [...Kimberly Zink] holds nothing back as she allows readers to unwrap the story of her life to watch her find the hidden treasures that changed her future and, if you're willing to go through your own self-discovery, can also change yours." —Kristie Powers

"*KIMBERLY'S STORY* certainly could be a victim story, yet it is a display of an uncommon victory that many humans never find. In her raw uncovering of the historical facts of her life, she teaches and models the power to choose and overcome those hurtful and darker places we all face. Kimberly's truth bearing and truth finding are inspiring." —Jenny Price

"*THIS IS* Kimberly Zink at her best. She shares the painful story of her early life, along with how she overcame her circumstances to become the woman she is today." —Reuben Romandy

"*I LOVE Me Not . . . I Love Me . . .* is a heart-wrenching, vulnerable memoir of the transformation of Kimberly Zink from unwanted and unloved to loved, valued, and cherished." —Jeff Meier

"*THIS BOOK* is an inspiring experiential journey that guides us through every step of overcoming and thriving after some of life's most challenging obstacles. Kimberly shares from the heart and is a true gift to humanity." —Kathy Fairbanks, radio host, VoiceAmerica

"*IN MY* thirty-five-year career, I have yet to work with anyone more authentic than Kimberly Zink. As you read her incredible story of the many obstacles she has overcome, you will realize that it is possible to tell a 'different' story and be the positive difference to others. This is a great book for anyone regardless of his or her circumstances." —Pam Cross

"*I WAS* immediately captivated by real-life events delivered in a frank and honest way. This account of horrific abuse and Kimberly Zink's courage to overcome is inspirational to all who seek more joyful, fulfilling lives."—Diane Beinschroth

"*KIMBERLY HAS* mentored and coached me and many others through our darkest places. In this book and in her life, Kimberly truly shares her heart. She is willing to step into her darkness to make someone else's becoming a shade or two lighter and gives evidence to the world that there is choice and hope no matter the circumstance."—Tiyana Sample, teen mentor

"*I LOVE Me Not . . . I Love Me . . .* is raw, real, and riveting. Kimberly Zink is courageous and steadfast and is part of God's fierce revolution for the soul. She has put into words the incredible power of forgiveness and truly loving oneself."—Sheva Nickravesh

"*THIS MUST-READ* book details the inspiration that is Kimberly Zink, a courageous woman who experienced years of neglect, abuse, violence, and rape from the time she was a little girl. Successful by any definition of the word, Kimberly is a shining example of a Compassionate Samurai: a true warrior with a servant's heart who has touched thousands of lives and literally saved many of them."—Mike Coviello

"*KIMBERLY ZINK'S* fearless authenticity and bold compassion have increased my self-awareness. Journey with her through *I Love Me Not . . . I Love Me . . .* and may true liberty be yours forever!"—Tony Dunn, pastor, New Day Christian Fellowship, Corona, California

"*THIS BOOK* is about truth. Amazing honesty and recovery. Here's to living our best lives no matter what we've been through."—Debra Haines, owner, Clar8ty

"*KIMBERLY ZINK* boldly shares her life and the choices she made to move from bitter to become better. Thankfully, she found hope in God and the principles taught by Brian Klemmer. Make a great choice to implement the principles from this book!"—Brenton Dearing, president, Wealth Ambassadors; author of *God's Eye Is on the Sparrow*

"*I LOVE Me Not . . . I Love Me . . .* can help you create much more joy and peace in your life. Go with Kimberly on this journey of love, forgiveness, and creation."—Jennifer Kwan

"*KIMBERLY ZINK* pours her life experience into this book, from a place of hurt and anguish to a space of true love for her authentic self and a compassion for others. For those who have ever struggled with self-love and self-worth, this is certainly a book to connect with."—Eric McHugh

"*THIS BOOK* is an in-depth account of how a beautiful but lost soul fought to turn her circumstances into experiences that drove her to not be another statistic and instead strive to be her best and help others find that strength as well."—Jeannie Holehan Holm, real estate agent

"*WITHOUT A* doubt, a must-read for all ages. Kimberly Zink never disappoints with her commitment, heart, and truth. She defines survivor, and my world is better with her in my life."—Bob Howard, US Marine Corps (retired)

"*KIMBERLY IS* one of those people you meet who brings light into your world as soon as you meet her, and she does precisely that with this book. *I Love Me Not . . . I Love Me . . .* shows how to dispel the darkness and bring that very same light." —James Hannan

"*KIMBERLY ZINK* shares her intimately beautiful and gracefully honest journey in *I Love Me Not . . . I Love Me . . .*. Her story will undoubtedly inspire courage and evoke passionate determination for all readers. Her powerful messages of choice, moving forward despite all odds, and the resiliency of the human spirit transcend generations and speaks to the humanity in us all." —Kayla Fox, student counselor and educator

"*KIMBERLY ZINK* shares her soul in this book for the purpose of inspiring others to dig deep, heal, and become whole again. She helps transform lives and will continue on that journey with this powerful and authentic piece of work." —Tasreen Khamisa, executive director, Tariq Khamisa Foundation

"*A TRULY* empowering book with a great perspective on love that inspires you to give the best while achieving the love you deserve." —Claes Lindholm, investment capitalist

"*KIMBERLY'S STORY* is powerful and captivating. Days after reading it, I am still exploring what it tells us about the human condition. She's a brave storyteller." —Carl Nordgren, novelist; educator; entrepreneur

"*GOD BLESS* Kimberly's honesty and transparency in her amazing, heartfelt book. My hope is that readers will come to know that they too can be more than a survivor and be truly victorious by guiding others to change their lives for the better."—Mary Robb, business owner

"**Kimberly Zink** has opened her heart and shared her knowledge and expertise in order to change the world and empower others to do the same. Her desire to share the teachings of Brian Klemmer with others has truly affected me in a way I could never have imagined. I strongly encourage you to experience Kimberly's book. It will show you how she has lived these teachings to change her life and the lives of thousands of leaders."
—Roni Rumsey, Isagenix distributor

"**In her** book, Kimberly speaks to healing and restoration on the other side of the darkness of abuse. She reveals the power of forgiveness, meaning, and love in the midst of deep loss and pain. Innocence can be restored. Love does save the day."—Melinda Estefano Indahl

"**A riveting** testament of the human spirit. Kimberly lays it all on the line how she triumphed in the face of unthinkable torment."—Toby Fisher

"**Written by** a woman who, by all indications, would be a hopeless statistic of abuse and youth gone awry yet, through her dogged and passionate pursuit of healing and wholeness, was transformed to a life of purpose and contribution. A painfully honest read, this will empower those challenged by abuse and injustice to realize that truly anything is possible!"—David Knight

"**Up from** the ashes of abuse and despair, the story of a modern day heroine—one who has experienced first hand that, truly *anything IS possible! An honest and powerful read."—Anita Knight

"*COMPELLING TO* the core of the heart. A resounding triumph as in the teaching of great love found in Corinthians."—Ruby Muza

"*I LOVE Me Not . . . I Love Me . . .* paints a picture of a beautiful soul who survived and even thrived in spite of horrific pain and tragedy. Kimberly is raw, authentic, and passionate about helping people discover that no matter what happens to us, it is how we choose to perceive it that will allow us to rise above even our worst nightmares. This book is a journey of hope, survival, transformation, and heart, and you will never be the same once you read it."—Suzette Teague, real estate broker

"*KIMBERLY HAS* done an amazing job following in the footsteps of Brian Klemmer for leading K&A, and I wholeheartedly support her. Written from the heart, her book is a testament to her resiliency and wisdom and will help many young women."—Azim Khamisa

"*A POWERFUL* message for a generation often defined by brokenness. It offers hope for anyone who is fighting to break free from the inertia of past sins."—Glenn Arakawa

"*KIMBERLY IS* the embodiment of the quote 'The hottest fire makes the strongest steel.' With this book, she uses her life lessons to show us how to live with more passion, love, and purpose. She is a gifted teacher of thousands and now reaches many more with her new book. Highly recommended!"—Tom Kenemore

"*THERE ARE* people in this world who can enter a space and instantly connect in the full spectrum of human existence. Kimberly Zink is one of those people. The experiences she shares in this book are not only a testament to her transformation but also a guide to those who are willing to follow." —Richard Stevenson

"*POWERFUL. MOVING.* Inspiring. Kimberly proves that you can not only overcome any obstacle but also come out on the other end unscathed, loving deeper and truer than ever imaginable." —Robbie Campbell

"*A COMPELLING* ride of truth about choices. Kimberly's authentic insights make this a handbook of actionable empowerment. Buy this book and read it like a roast dinner, chewing every choice." —Annette Cosgrove

"*KIMBERLY ZINK* is an empowering, bold, and beautiful woman. I am forever touched by the love she has shown me just by being courageous enough to be honest and compassionate. I hope this book challenges you to realize you are more than enough." —Jessica Woods

"*KIMBERLY IS* a truth teller, and I highly endorse her and her book. You will be enlightened, encouraged, and blessed as you read it." —Jerry Priore

"*WHEN YOU* read this book, you'll experience Kimberly Zink's personal journey from surviving to thriving. By applying the principles she shares, you'll avoid the pitfalls and land mines of life and enjoy more of your own personal thriving. This book is a must-read!" —Kieran Murry, author of *Go For Your Gold*

"*KIMBERLY ZINK* shares her gut-level honesty and love with people in her seminar rooms and again in this book. As she shares her life experiences and revelations, she helps others learn how just changing the meaning they have attached to events can truly change their lives." —Beth Harvey

"*KIMBERLY, THANKS* for sharing your vulnerable lessons. You have been able to share your heart very clearly and concisely through your coaching leadership with Klemmer as well as translate those lessons into written words. This is not easy to do. You write with heart and eloquence, and I'm excited that your words on the page will most certainly empower many more people on this planet." —Stephen Erickson

"*EVERYONE HAS* a story. Some stories are sad. Some are thrilling. This one is exceptional! Kimberly Zink shatters the silence and breaks down the walls about a subject that has been kept secret too long. Child molestation: will anyone listen, care, or understand? Will anyone believe me? These are very real questions. Learn how one lonely little girl overcame the trauma, stigma, and soul-wrenching guilt and pain as she sought to find the true meaning of love." —Susan Holsinger

"*WORDS CANNOT* describe the positive impact Kimberly Zink will have upon you. She skillfully shares her deepest and darkest moments and turns them into a positive that will help inspire countless people. Well done!" —Dr. Terrence Young

"*KIMBERLY BRINGS* to her book what she brings in person: the raw truth. In *I Love Me Not . . . I Love Me . . .*, you'll find an honest and vulnerable example of what life can look like when you choose to go beyond circumstances, create new meanings, and authentically love yourself." —Thom Mills

"*SHARING HOPE* and encouragement, Kimberly Zink bravely rips back the veil that concealed a lifetime of brokenness and sexual abuse." —Kevin Trim

I LOVE ME NOT...
I LOVE ME...

David,

Your a gift, to a world that is in pain! You using the tools will support the rest of us win as well! You are a powerful, worthy, and deserving man!

I Love Me Not...
I Love Me...

by
Kimberly Zink

I Love Me Not . . . I Love Me . . .

Copyright © 2016 by Kimberly Zink
All rights reserved.
Reproduction in any form without permission is prohibited.

Every attempt has been made to protect the privacy of those who were involved in the narrative of this story. Details such as names, ages, cities, references, and circumstances have been changed whenever possible. The facts presented and written about my life's experiences are true to my words and reactions without disrespect intended to anyone in the process.

ISBN-13: 978-0-692-77669-8

Printed in the United States of America
1 2 3 4 5 6 7 8 / 20 19 18 17 16

Dedication

THIS BOOK is dedicated first to Tim Zink and my family now and my family then. I am grateful for each and every choice that got us *all* here.

Next, I want to thank each member of the Klemmer & Associates organization for being the Compassionate Samurai you truly are, and each student for being open and willing to create a world that works for everyone with no one left out. This book would not exist without the commitment of Brian Klemmer, who started K&A out of passion and integrity. The tools the company offers are powerful and healing to all who will receive them.

Finally, I dedicate this book to everyone who has been part of my preparation for greatness. Your influence was of love, respect, and loyalty while others influenced me through violence, betrayal, lack of integrity, lies, and pain. With my whole heart I say thank you. God used each experience to teach, stretch, and mold me into the woman he needed to do his bidding.

Contents

Foreword by Jim Stovall 17
Introduction 19

One
SOMEONE WILL TEACH YOU 25

Two
I JUST WANTED YOU TO BE PROUD 35

Three
SEVEN STEPS TO LIBERTY 45

Four
GOD KNOWS WHAT HE'S DOING 53

Five
ARMOR FOR THE WOUNDED 63

Six
A PRISON OF MY OWN MAKING 73

Seven
A LITTLE WINE GOES A LONG WAY 87

Eight
I CAN'T REMEMBER WHEN… 99

Nine
DO YOU WANT TO HAVE A LIFE? 111

About the Author 121

Foreword

Dear Reader:

As the author of thirty books with six of my titles having been turned into movies, I have long believed that if you can tell a great story, you earn the right to share your message. Within these pages, my friend and colleague Kimberly Zink is going to share her story, and I am confident that you will agree with me that Kimberly has earned the right to share her message. Kimberly's story is painful and tragic but also triumphant and victorious. One of my favorite authors, Louis L'Amour, often shared that a person can be judged only against the backdrop of the time and place in which he or she lived. Kimberly has lived through torment that few of us can imagine, but she has emerged to make a contribution to the world that few of us can equal.

I met Kimberly Zink, as I meet countless people around the world, after one of my speaking engagements. She told me that first night that someday she would be working for the organization that had hired me to speak at that particular event. Today I am pleased to tell you that I have spoken at approximately forty events for that organization, Klemmer & Associates, and Kimberly now serves as their chief executive officer. Anyone seeing Kimberly today would be impressed with all she has done and the heights she has achieved, but her success becomes even more poignant when you understand her beginnings and the trials and ordeals she has faced.

I know that it is not easy for Kimberly to share some of the candid episodes you are going to read within this book, but I know her heart and spirit and am convinced that she is willing to share her scars so you and I can attain even greater success in our own lives.

I often tell my readers and those to whom I speak that you should never take advice from anyone who doesn't have what you want. We all have dealt with obstacles and residual garbage from our pasts. I can think of no better guide to lead us out of the wilderness and into the Promised Land than Kimberly Zink.

I hope this book will be just the beginning of your relationship of discovery and success with Kimberly. I hope you will explore the opportunity to engage more deeply with her through the events at Klemmer & Associates. If you will take advantage of this path that Kimberly is offering, I believe you will emerge into a bright new world that will exceed your wildest expectations.

Read, experience, and grow.

Jim Stovall
Best-selling author of *The Ultimate Gift*

Introduction

*Every day, the story you tell yourself, the story you believe,
is exactly the one you will live. It's your choice.*

LIFE HAPPENS. Every moment of every hour, the good, the bad, the ugly, and the beautiful are happening all around us. We all have experiences in life—whether random, planned, or orchestrated—that fill our days, weeks, and years.

These things that we experience in our *lives*—the places we go, the people we meet, the events that occur (whether we participate or are merely witnesses)—I will call *facts*. Some facts are perceived as good, and others as bad. But what makes us unique and amazing individuals is that, regardless of what the facts are, we have a choice as to how we interpret the facts. We have the ability, in every moment, to choose our own stories. Even if we don't know we have choices, they are there. We have the choice to assign meaning—negative or positive—to each one of those facts. It is a gift we all possess.

Here's what I mean. As a child, I was sexually abused for twelve years. It is an undeniable fact that there was abuse. It happened and it was physical and sexual in nature. Some people would experience that same situation and say, "It was the worst experience of my life." "It stole my innocence." "It ruined my life." "I must have done something wrong. I asked for it. It was my fault." Sadly, these are meanings that are quite common.

But on the other hand, there are people who have given that same fact very different meanings. "This happened and I can learn and use that experience to help people." "This happened and now I can empathize with others on a deeper level." "This happened and it gives me insight to support myself and others."

One fact, several different meanings. We get to choose.

Wait a minute, you may be thinking. *Which one is true?*

The answer is simple: *the one that you believe is true.* The meaning you believe is true for you is the truth you are creating moment by moment by moment. The story you are telling yourself is the story that now is your current reality. One choice creates meaning around one fact. All day, every day, we choose what we want to believe about what has happened and what is happening in our lives.

Example:

Choice A: If I choose to believe that I was abused because I was dirty, filthy, and unwanted, I will make decisions based on this belief—based on those thoughts and patterns. I will even prove that my belief is right and create more evidence in my life that I am dirty and filthy and unwanted.

Choice B: If I choose to believe that I was abused because my abuser did not know any other way, that he had likely been abused in the same way, that he chose me because I was special and valued, then I matter and my life will bear evidence that I am special and valued. To be clear, this doesn't mean he had an excuse. It simply gives me a choice of what energy I give my experience: hate or misunderstanding or seeking of love.

Regardless of whether I think thoughts that are positive, true, and serving or thoughts that are negative, false, and destructive, they are my story to tell. They are my story to live. Either way, what happened really happened. The facts are what they are, and sexual abuse took place. But the choice of how to define the event is mine. The meanings I create are making my life what it is. The meaning behind the fact is completely up to me. How I use my story to create my experience is my choice and mine alone.

Now, I am not suggesting that I created the event that happened. I am not saying that my thoughts brought this abuse into my life. I was an innocent participant in this event. But my power as a human being with free will and free choice is that I get to decide what I am going to make this mean, in this moment and the next.

One of the gifts I have been given is the opportunity to test this numerous times. Many life-altering "facts" have happened in my short life. What I choose to make them mean now is what I get to teach thousands of others every year in my work with Klemmer & Associates. I share my story because this is what I believe works: the practice of choice around our past in order to create our present and our future.

Years ago I had meanings that I had created around the facts of my life. I let them be the deciding factors of why I could not succeed. I let them determine why I didn't deserve to have good things or a wonderful life. How could someone like me—a dirty, unloved, broken girl—get to have a good life? How could I have any blessings after all the terrible things that happened to me? How could I have happiness, wealth, and a great family?

・・・

This book you hold in your hands is the completion of a project that the mentors in my life requested I write, as well as thousands of students who asked me to share my story for them and others they wanted to support. I wrote this book with every intention to, above all, do *no* harm.

This isn't a drama-filled revenge play. *I have changed every detail possible about names, ages, cities, references, and circumstances to protect the privacy of those who were involved in the narrative of my story.* I have written about my life's experiences true to my words and reactions but without disrespecting anyone in the process. My recall of memories comes from the wounds of an unhealed girl. My anger, pain, joy, and surrender can be felt in my words. I am simply allowing an opportunity to heal myself and others.

All of us have lingering memories from the past that have to be dealt with in the present if we are going to address our full potentials in the future. What if this would work for you? What if it were possible in your life? What if you could leave behind the victim mentality for good? The good news is you can! I wrote this book for you, and I wrote it for me. It has helped me realize how far I have come and how beautifully long my future is and all the great works left to be done. Many more mistakes and events have and will occur that I get to transform into leverage and lessons.

I perceived myself as a victim. That was my story. That was the Kimberly I created. If anyone, especially me, needed any explanation or justification for why my life was not what it should be or what I said I wanted it to be, I could point to all the horrible facts and say, "See! It's not my fault. I had no choice. Look at what was *done to me*. I never had a chance."

But what if . . . ? What if you get to decide? In this book, I will share my story in the hope that even one of the facts or events of my life may resonate—may be what you need to hear to set your life on a very different path. I am grateful today—not for the events actually occurring, but for what I have learned. The point is this: I learned that I can change my present and my future if I will just learn from my past. I have the power to create the person I am committed to being and the life I want to have. And so do you.

One

SOMEONE WILL TEACH YOU

LITTLE GIRLS don't know what love is. Someone has to teach them.

Every little girl needs a daddy and as a little girl, I was no different. But my daddy was gone. He left to go live his own life because he and Momma couldn't get along. Little girls don't know what love is, especially when their daddy leaves and shows up for only guilt-driven visitations.

My mom did the best she could, especially since she had no one to show her how to be a mother.

"Kimberly, go to bed! Kimberly, be quiet, honey. Momma's tired. Kimberly, please! Just go to your room. You're a big girl—you'll figure it all out."

My mom needed help with us kids, I needed time and attention, and what seemed like the perfect solution to our situation lived right next door.

George was a neighbor teen who wanted to make some extra cash.

Momma needed a reliable sitter, and if help was ever needed, his family was close by, so it totally made sense.

So off we went. George played with me in a new and very personal way. He made me feel as though I mattered. He was safe, funny, strong, and most of all, he liked me.

I was too young to meet George at his bus stop, but every day I would sit at home waiting at the top of the stairs, perfectly still and quiet, hoping and longing for George to come and see me. Some days he came. Some days he didn't. But when he did, I felt loved. We were together intimately, and I belonged.

I Love Me Not . . .

When I got a little older, I asked George why we always had to do this. It hurt physically and wasn't fun, yet his answer made me forget all that. When George said, "This is what you do when you love someone," I believed him.

Finally, in a moment it all made sense: sex equaled love. The more that happened, the more he would love me.

George spoke words of comfort that I longed to hear: "Kimberly, I chose you. You are so special to me. This is what we get to share because I chose you."

I believed him.

Little girls don't know what love is. Someone has to teach them. George promised I was his, which meant someone wanted me; someone cared if I was alive. Therefore I sought it, fought for it, thought about it all day long—because for me, that was the only time I felt connected, loved, and wanted.

I still didn't know what love was. Not really.

I Love Me Not . . .

I still remember the day George left for college. I was heartbroken. I knew that I would be alone now and that the only person who loved me, George, the one who promised and gave me love (because sex equaled love), must not love me anymore or he wouldn't leave—just like my dad did (because leaving meant I was not loved). I was right back where I started: unwanted, unsafe, unloved.

Little girls don't know what love is. Someone has to teach them.

I learned that men love you and then men leave. *So, don't attach, Kimberly,* I told myself. *Just connect when you can, get what you can, and then shut down when it is "over." Love won't last. It never does. No matter how much you give, do, hope, love doesn't last forever.*

When it's based on a physical act versus a heart-to-heart connection, it simply can't.

I didn't understand. Sadness, pain, confusion, disappointment, and hopelessness filled my world more and more every day.

. . .

That first year of George being away at college was dreadfully long. He had been gone all fall and spring when my mother came to me and told me that George wanted to come to our house for the summer. I was so excited to have him back in my life, even if it were only for a short time.

When he finally arrived, the sexual connection started up all over again, as I had expected and wanted—literally hoped for—day after day during that lonely year. I wasn't a little girl anymore—I was a *big* girl and I believed I had been saved by George. We were connected. *Now that he's back,* I thought, *it will be like old times. He will love me again!* Which meant I was loveable again. Until, one day, everything changed.

George invited his friend Richard to stay with us for a few days. Momma saw it as harmless, so with no place to stay, Richard was invited into our home.

That night my mom was gone and everyone else was asleep, so just like so many times before, George came to my room to get me. He sent me to the master bedroom, so I hurried down the hall, took off all my clothes, and got under the covers to wait for him.

What happened next shattered my world. Richard got into bed with us. I didn't know what was happening, but I knew it was all wrong. I looked up at George's face in confusion.

George said it would be okay. "It just means more love." It was the first time I could see that George was lying. I decided love must include lies, as well as sex and abandonment.

I couldn't speak, but my eyes cried out, "George, you made me think this was special. Something only we shared. Why is he here? Why is this so loud and scary? George, you said *you* loved me and *you* would take care of me. *Why?*"

But because I trusted George, I went along with his requests—all of them, just as I had for so many years. Yet after that night, I knew that love was a lie. It was painful and lonely. Love hurt. Love left. Love used. Love wanted what it wanted.

Little girls don't know what love is. They have to be taught. That night George taught me that I wasn't special and that I didn't really matter at all. And if this were really love, I wasn't so sure I wanted it. The confusion was blinding, torturous, degrading, yet presented as a gift. I didn't understand.

I Love Me Not . . .

I left that chapter of George behind when I moved to a new town with my family. But sadly and tragically, the longing for attention and love—as I had been taught to define it—created a space for another young and curious boy to take up right where George had left off. Lucky me—or so I thought.

This began a toxic pattern in my life of looking for love in all the wrong places. Over the next several years, I sought love in the moment, only to be cast aside by each boy or man I met. Whether I received attention for thirty minutes or a decade, given enough time, it died. Each experience was more degrading and dirty than the last and I was devalued all the more—every single time it happened, hundreds of times over.

But I was determined to do whatever it took to create the opportunity to get the attention I needed and wanted so desperately. Then I would fight hard to keep it—so I would matter.

I became the girl who parents didn't want their kids to be around. I was on the receiving end of many colorful labels, such as "slut," "whore," and "white trash"—both out in the world and inside my own home.

The girls in my school hated me because I was a threat to the attention they were looking for from boys. Even the good boys—the nice boys—were vulnerable to being seduced, because I had the power. After all, I'd learned from the best. Love is sex. So give them more. I was lost and alone when I gave sex or attention in hopes of receiving love. Instead, I received only hate and disgust.

The few girlfriends I had also eventually turned their backs on me because of my actions, and understandably so. Sure, to my face they said one thing, but behind my back it was another story. I was unwelcome in their circle. I had a few friends who cared for me and tried to protect me against all the judgment, but even with them in my corner, I felt stressed, lost, and all alone. I hated that no one—not even me—understood my heart, my thinking, or my actions.

Fact = Meaning—the Moment of Shift!

These are the *facts* of my early years, but more important was the *meaning* that I perceived about these events. Because I believed that men love you, use you, steal from you, and then leave, just like my father and just like George, then *I could not have been lovable.* I believed I was unworthy of joy and therefore *I did not deserve to be happy.* I believed I was bad—even evil—and therefore *even God didn't want me.* I believed I was dirty and therefore *I was not acceptable.* I believed I was trash and therefore *I was not desirable to anyone.* I believed I was broken, so there was no chance things would turn out well for me and *I would never be successful.*

I Love Me . . .

With a lot of support and understanding from people who believed in me (thank you!), I finally got it. Love is not just sex; it's not simply physical. It is not taking, stealing, intentionally using or manipulating without remorse. Love is not a "have to" or a "need to." Love isn't mean, belittling, or fearful. Love isn't a lie or a trap. Love doesn't lie to you or about you.

Love is passionate. Love is silly. Love is quiet and giving, because love is a heart-to-heart connection. Love doesn't pursue only to take from another; love pursues because of all it can give. Love always produces more love, more giving, more life. Love is intimate, safe, and stable because of what love pours into another, not because of what it takes.

This was a completely different paradigm from what I had experienced and defined myself by for so long. I finally began healing through years of trust building, intimacy choosing, and the releasing of what was—what never was love in the first place. Healing does come—*when it is chosen!*

I decided my new truth about love: *Love is honoring myself and others. Love is not an act; it's an action. Love is not selfish. Love is for giving and for-giving. Love is about creation, not destruction. Love is of light, not darkness.*

I chose to change my view of the facts. I chose to question—and then redefine—everything that I had experienced. I chose to create new meaning for all the facts, and that would change my life forever.

I Love Me . . .

What George did to me, someone else had done to George, for this type of abuse tends to be passed down from abused to abused. What abusers do to the abused, they learned somewhere on their own paths. At one time they too were the unvalued, the uncherished. This isn't an excuse; it's awareness accompanied by grace through my eyes today.

Ultimately, it's my choice what I believe about the meaning behind the facts of my life, and it's a choice I make all day long. Some days it's every moment, and some days the victories last longer.

I choose to "love me" even when feelings of ugliness pop up—even when the words "You're a slut" reverberate in my memory. I choose to "love me" when I make devastating mistakes, am unappreciative of others, or withhold myself needlessly. I choose to "love me" even when someone tells me I'm no good or not worth it and when the voices whisper, "They're just gonna leave. They only love you because they want something. Don't trust them; they will hurt you."

I choose to "love me" even when the words won't come; even when the guilt (of all the mistakes I have made) eats at me and my heart is bruised and sore; even when those who love me well, who love me best, don't meet my expectations. Even then I choose to "love me" because *I can choose.*

A NOTE TO YOU:

For many years, the meaning of love was sex. Today the meaning of love is human connection at a heart level. Love doesn't have to be calls, visits, stuff. Love never stops or starts; it's constantly in flow. It's simply a willingness to receive or give out of the flow. Today I love thousands and am loved by thousands, not through performing but by being; not by telling people what they *want* to hear but by saying what they *need* to hear; not by manipulation but through authenticity; not by selling out but instead by honoring my spirit and valuing myself; not by feeling I'm being punished but by choosing to be grateful for being prepared.

It is also your choice—no matter what was, what is, or what will be in your life. Love is what you define it to be: sex or heart connection. You get to decide. Abundantly believe you can have it all.

OLD

FACT		MEANING
SEXUAL ACTIVITY	=	LOVE
DO EXTRA STUFF	=	NEED ME
FOLLOW ALL THE RULES	=	I AM A GOOD GIRL
TAKE CARE OF OTHERS	=	I AM A GOOD GIRL

NEW

FACT		MEANING
SEXUAL ACTIVITY	=	A MECHANISM TO EXPRESS CONNECTION TO A LOVER
DO EXTRA STUFF	=	I AM CAPABLE, AND IT IS AN OPPORTUNITY TO SERVE OTHERS
FOLLOW ALL THE RULES	=	DO MY BEST TO ADD TO STRUCTURE FOR COMFORT AND SAFETY
TAKE CARE OF OTHERS	=	OPPORTUNITY TO SUPPORT, MAKE A CONTRIBUTION

Two
I JUST WANTED YOU TO BE PROUD

NO CHILD wants to grow up without a father around, and I was no different. I was the little girl who imagined how amazing it would be to have a "daddy." All of my friends who had a daddy seemed happy, loved, and complete.

If I had taken a snapshot of my world, joy, love, and complete didn't exist. Sexual abuse, my parents' divorce, being the oldest child, and being seen as troubled only made the effects of having an uninvolved father all the more daunting.

To her credit, my mother would rarely speak poorly of my father. When I asked questions and wanted to know details about why he left, she would say that they just weren't happy and had different paths, which caused them to fight all the time. But she never said she hated him or griped about his character flaws. If anything, she seemed disappointed that he didn't *want* to take responsibility for me financially or emotionally. He did what the legal paperwork instructed, and little more in my child eyes.

Conversely, throughout my childhood, my dad would justify his position using reasons why he couldn't get along with my mom. He spoke often of his frustration with my mother and would say things like "She spent all my money" or "She is a silly, hopeless start-upper" or "She's just being spoiled and expects too much." There was no question my dad was unhappy with my mom and, of course, that had to be why he left: he didn't love her. Right? As a child, I didn't understand how relationships worked. All I knew was that ours wasn't working.

I Love Me Not . . .

When I was really young, my dad lived two blocks away from me, yet he rarely interacted with me. I think at some level he just didn't know how, but I didn't understand. He rarely spent time with me. He appeared scared to show me physical affection. He didn't demonstrate that he was excited to be with me or that I was worth his time. Through my little girl eyes, I felt like an inconvenience and a burden.

I would see other men with their kids and would compare them to what my father did—what I wanted him to be doing, but wasn't. It only made me feel emptier. I would make up outlandish ideas about all the disappointments.

If he loved me, he would want to be with me.

If he loved me, he would love me like a daddy, not leave me exposed to George's kind of "love."

If he loved me, he would come see me in sports.

If he loved me . . . on and on.

Well, my father never met my expectations, desires, or dreams, so obviously he didn't love me, or at least that was how I saw it with my child eyes.

Many times I would be stretching before a soccer game, imagining my dad's truck parking and him walking across the grass to the sidelines. Rarely, if ever, would he come, and if he did he would show up late. If I had a bad game, he wouldn't make any effort to address it or say anything to cheer me up. He wouldn't say a word. So I thought, *If he loved me, he would say something. If only I mattered. If only I could be a good enough soccer player . . . student . . . daughter. . . .*

If only I could be different, maybe, just maybe, he could be proud of me.

As I got older, I would call him and ask if I could go see him. Sometimes he said yes out of guilt. Sometimes he said yes because the girls he dated wanted him to be more fatherly. It seemed to me that he came to get me only to show them he was a good person—that he cared.

A weekend with him was scripted. He would pick me up Friday night. Saturday morning was chocolate doughnuts and chocolate milk and WWF wrestling on TV. It was an AWESOME way to not have to talk. Then I would go watch him do a sport. He was a great athlete and did all kinds of different sports. I particularly remember bowling and baseball. We'd go out for fast food that night and then he would take me home on Sunday. Mostly the activities were enjoyable and designed to avoid all unwanted connection and conversation. We both were like trapped rats wanting out. We were both scared of each other, doing it wrong, needing to be liked, feeling unworthy of love. We were truly doing the best we could with what we had.

Sometimes there was a woman involved—sometimes a woman and her family. They were all very nice people. But as much as my dad tried, his relationships never worked out for very long.

I Love Me Not...

The hardest thing to bear was that my siblings had a dad present in their lives.

My mom was married a couple times and the other kids had dads who were there for them on a much larger scale.

My sister had her dad in our house. He treated her special; she was his little girl.

My brother's dad would take him to the lake and even keep him for weeks at a time over the summer. They seemed happy.

Both of them were wanted, loved, valued, included, and I was not.

My dad had little, if any, active role in my life. He rarely came through in all the areas I thought I needed him most, like attending sports events, my first car, prom—basic kid desires. He didn't know how to talk to me. He didn't understand me. I made him nervous. And as I grew older, I was becoming a lot like the woman who raised me—the woman he left. I became a walking, talking reminder of the past and reopened some old wounds. My becoming like my mother seemed to terrify him. He was honest about his disapproval of my mother and would follow it up with, "And you are acting just like her!" (Just what every teenager wants to hear.)

Through my parents words and actions, I believed that I was created out of hate, not love. After all, my dad made it clear he disapproved of my mother. I even rebelled against my mom to try to get my dad to love me. I had seen only disrespect between them, for themselves and for each other. And I am "them," which meant I was twice as much hate. The hardest thing about all this was that I believed I was created out of "the dark." So it was no wonder I made my mom sick her entire pregnancy and my dad angry enough to eventually leave. I destroyed them. So I couldn't blame him for not being willing to be there for me. He'd left me mentally, emotionally, physically, and spiritually for his own survival—or at least this is how I felt.

I Love Me . . .

It's been this way for years. Even now, forty years later, we exchange the occasional card—no more, no less. We hadn't spoken for nearly eight years until recently, when my dad called to tell me about my brother-in-law passing away. I didn't really know this brother-in-law, but for my dad, this was a connection. For him to take the time and to be so uncomfortable yet still call was reaching out in his own way. I am truly grateful.

Fortunately, I have given new meaning to all of the facts of my relationship with my father. In my experience, my dad was analytical and very closed down emotionally and physically. He seemed to suffer from anxiety and took few risks. He appeared sheltered and on guard, and while he had a strong work ethic, he never seemed to be having fun. He didn't know how to cut loose and experience joy. I never once saw him relax around me.

Ironically, my mom was exactly the opposite. She knew how to play and have fun. She was very much willing to put herself out there and take risks, even silly ones. She was also very in tune with her emotions; she was extremely emotional and experienced her feelings on a deep level.

Obviously, all these differences were the very things that attracted my dad to my mom and why he wanted her in the first place. He fell in love with my mom for all the things he didn't have and vice versa, and this is why they married and had a baby. He wanted to be all those things that she was and she did the same with him, and out of that "love connection" they created me.

My dad and my mom truly wanted to be complete. I was conceived when they were in this place of combining all possibilities.

Unfortunately, neither of them had the tools to know that was not the way to become whole. They were unknowingly using one another rather than being complete within themselves. They were doing the best they could with what they had.

After their divorce, my developing many of my mother's attributes reminded my dad of all those things he didn't have. I believe it created sadness in him. When he looked at me, he saw all the things he didn't feel he was. It wasn't that he didn't love me or like me; it was that I was and still am everything that was not part of his journey early on in life. I intimidated him. My experience, my view of events, my feelings were so different from his that it overwhelmed him. I have learned that different is good.

Fact = Meaning—the Moment of Shift

I was born out of an intention, an action, and a desire for completion. I was the completing factor, even if my parents chose not to stay together long term. The best parts of both my parents are in me.

As I learned to self-love a bit at a time, I realized that I have the best and worst parts of these two people, which combined makes a third: *me*. It is my responsibility to mine for the diamonds in my own backyard and develop the gifts and talents I inherited, not focus on what I lack. We can all three be very different. We can now take what we want and leave the rest.

A NOTE TO YOU:

You may remember earlier in this chapter I mentioned that my father called me to tell me about my brother-in-law's death. It was a sad yet wonderful conversation. I asked about Gary and his life to simply catch up on years missed. My father spent some time talking about Gary's accomplishments and success, both personal and professional. He shared that Gary had specialized in a system that allowed him to travel the world and share with thousands of people. He was a facilitator who helped people, and the company he worked for respected him and treated him like family. Then my dad said, "He was a good person who was loved very much because he helped so many people. Gary took good care of his family, so they will be fine. I was honored to know him; I am so proud of him."

Once I picked my jaw up off the ground, I took a deep breath and put my hand over the receiver and said, "Okay, God, I get it!" He had just described me and my life almost to the letter.

In that moment, I learned that my father is proud of a person who does the type of things I do. Therefore, I get to choose to know at a heart level that I may never hear those words from him about me. It's okay; that day I did! I was open to it looking different than I'd expected and I received it with joy. I pray for Gary's family with hope and love, and I know that God used him to help heal me.

Today my biological father is the proud husband of a wonderful woman who shared two beautiful, successful daughters with him. He has grandchildren who are blessed to have him in their lives. I am very happy for the love and support they have created and experienced as a family. My father found his family and led them as a mighty man of God.

I am so grateful for the space my father created by following his dream and not being in my active environment, because it made room for people who have come into my life to stand in roles of leadership, mentorship, and connection. Thomas L. Weeks, Patrick Dean, Brian Klemmer, Jim Stovall, Scott Pullan, and my "daddy," Brian J. Everhard, are all men who have respected me, taught me what to do and what not to do, helped prepare me for my future, and loved me even when I wasn't so lovable. I am grateful for all the guidance I have received. Thank you!

OLD

FACT		MEANING
FATHER NOT IN HOME	=	HE MUST NOT WANT ME
FATHER NOT AT EVENTS	=	HE IS EMBARRASSED BY ME
THE KID WITH NO DAD	=	I AM TRASH, SO HE DIDN'T WANT TO BE WITH ME

NEW

FACT		MEANING
FATHER NOT IN HOME	=	HE WAS FOLLOWING HIS DREAM FOR LOVE AND ACCEPTANCE
FATHER NOT AT EVENTS	=	HE WAS WORKING AND DESIGNING HIS NEXT STEPS
THE KID WITH NO DAD	=	HE KNEW I WAS STRONG AND WOULD THRIVE; I'M HIS KID

Three

SEVEN STEPS TO LIBERTY

IT WAS my early years of high school. I was definitely not the most popular kid, but that didn't stop me from partying with the best of them at our football games. I liked to drink. Heck, let's be honest, I liked to be mentally unavailable, and this particular game was no exception.

I don't know who we played that night, but I spent the entire game indulging as I normally did. By the time the game was over, I was already in party mode. Due to an argument with a friend, I decided not to go with my group and chose to head in a different direction.

I crossed the school complex where there was a group of people partying. There were seven guys hanging out. I knew them or at least of them, as it was a small town. They were partying and drinking, so I fit right in. They had beer to drink.

I never drank beer. I drank only wine coolers and liquor, but someone yelled out, "Hey, come on and have a beer with us!" The appeal was instantaneous—I was wanted—so I stayed and agreed to have that beer.

Somebody brought me a beer. It was already opened, so I threw my head back and drank it fast since it tasted awful to me. Within minutes, I got really woozy and silly. I didn't know what was happening to me; that wasn't my normal reaction to alcohol.

Very soon, the familiar noise of the crowd died down, even though many people who had come in from neighboring towns were still there. I was spinning, lost and out of control.

I completely blacked out.

I Love Me Not . . .

The rest of that night comes up in bits and pieces in my memory—shattered, icky pieces of a very dark story. I couldn't get a clear line of thought, only images of the evening: faces with shadows, and voices that I can still hear today but can't attach to anyone. Some faces are clear as crystal, yet I keep wanting to forget.

I remember being in the back bed of a truck and the sensation of my body lying there on the rigid wave lines, scooted all the way to end with parts of my body dangling.

My feet were tight, knees bent. My rear was right at the edge of the truck bed.

There was a group of guys laughing and talking, saying I was like a spittoon and they were filling me up! Lots of laughing and normal guy talk surrounded me.

I didn't fight or yell. It was as if I were inside myself and couldn't get out. I was trapped, so I just lay there and listened to all the different voices. There were times I felt as though I were outside of myself, looking back at this girl. I wanted to yell, I wanted to make them leave, yet I could do nothing.

Every so often they would pull me down, pick me up, and throw me back down on the bed of the truck, and the forcing, tearing, pulling, and hurting began again.

They would hold my legs up and just drop them down hard. It was so violent, yet not chaotic. They were doing whatever they wanted, however they wanted. Even now, the images are all raw.

It was as if I were paralyzed. The only thing I could control was my mind, but only moments at a time.

So I would look up and see the dark faces in the pitch black, the darkness all around me.

I remember looking around at them drinking and smoking and laughing, and they were taking turns.

One by one.

One after another, they would grab me, roll me over, and go again.

It seemed like it would never end.

I Love Me Not . . .

It was light outside when I woke up. I was on the ground and my clothes were disheveled. I looked around and saw I was lying in the dirt and grass.

And I was freezing.

Bits and pieces of what had happened to me came crashing into my consciousness.

I pulled myself up and could remember the things they'd said.

I decided to try to walk home. It was around sunrise, and as I trudged along the road, a policeman picked me up.

I didn't say a word. I was numb.

He dropped me off at my house and I walked inside, headed straight for the shower. I decided to spare my family, and told them that I was in a fight at a party. I felt they could handle that much better than the evil experience I endured.

After hiding for several days, I went back to school. I spent my time wandering and wondering, *Who?* I would look around and think, *Who was there?*

My mind played games with me. I would be sure I knew, and then I didn't. I doubted myself at every turn. I was sensitive to every loud noise, doors slamming.

When something like this happens, you always hear people say, "It's not your fault." Yet I saw it as *all* my fault. I saw myself as guilty for having been there and doing things that gave up my control. It was what I'd deserved. It was what they all knew I would do individually anyway, so why not do it all at the same time? It would do me no good to tell anyone, for who would believe the white-trash, slutty, evil, dirty girl? I remember thinking, *Accept that you deserved it. Everyone else already thinks so.*

Over the next couple of years, every time someone would look at me a certain way, I would wonder if they'd been there that night. As soon as I was "sure," doubt and confusion would creep in. I could never be completely sure.

Because of my past and the choices I'd made, what I believed about this situation was that I was scum of the earth. I was nothing more than a spittoon. The quality of my life didn't matter; I was worthy of exactly what I received that night. That night I'd heard that my body was no different than a hole in the mattress, so I might as well be put to some good use.

I had done so many things wrong that, in my mind, it was my fault. I basically believed I'd taught these guys that this was what to do with me. They knew they wouldn't get caught. No real consequences.

I Love Me . . .

The facts of this story are still the facts. I was at the game, I got into an argument, I went the other direction, I drank, and I was raped by seven different boys/men. I have described what I made each fact mean about me back then. I truly believed that I must have been evil and that is why God would let all these things happen to me. I was stained due to all of the sexual thoughts and actions and God was disappointed in me. Why would he protect the likes of me?

This was my truth for most of my life. It made perfect sense. Just what I've shared so far is a clear example. When I realized that no one has the power to make me feel a certain way, I started to dissect the feelings I had blamed all these men for. I laid my reaction and all the negative feelings I had at their feet. I didn't realize I had been giving away my power to choose. As long as it was about them and how they made me feel, they were still in control. I had created a meaning of how I would always be their victim. By doing that, I would never be my own person.

Fact = Meaning—the Moment of Shift

Just to be clear, I didn't create the rape, want the rape, or ask for the rape, yet I am responsible for how I react to it and how it affects my life. It was a bad situation and it created a lot of hurdles to overcome, such as depression, anxiety, panic attacks, fear, distrust, and the need to control. But today is different. Today I don't fear those boys/men; I feel sad for them. I know a couple of them from a distance and I can see the toll it has taken on them. They made a drunken, sad mistake that forever changed the eight of us. The blame, shame, and guilt they carry is hard to watch.

Today I understand group dynamics and how one angry person can lead others to hell. It's like watching a lamb being led to slaughter. Yet today I have faith because I've seen one peaceful, grounded, committed person stand in a room full of angry people and turn them and lead them to heaven. I have learned that living an unconscious life doesn't stop the pain; it just unsafely directs it.

A NOTE TO YOU:

I have been blessed to be a part of Klemmer Youth Leadership Camp for several years. I have laughed, cried, and grown from each child I've met there. My purpose in YLC is to help give the kids a chance to have these tools twenty years earlier than I found them. Less pain, less anger, less loss all motivate me to keep going.

There have been over a dozen young women and men over the years who have shared abuse or rape stories with me. They felt safe and understood when they confided in me. I have personally had a hand in helping them begin to heal and helping their families come together and support them. The love, acceptance of self, and forgiveness these girls have today are worth all I went through that night so long ago.

I have forgiven those boys/men, and continue to do it daily. I am not a saint or even a nice person all the time. I have lied, cheated, and stolen all my life to some degree or another. I have followed the angry man, I have stolen people's joy and light, and I have been unfaithful to those who loved me and faithful to many who hated me. I have stolen the innocence of many and added to the ego and pride of others. My point is that I acknowledge I have hurt others. Pain is pain, and no one is above sin.

The only difference today is I know there is a difference. I am able to become aware of my mistakes fairly quickly and do my best to correct my actions. Today I am aware it is my responsibility to take the action that brings about forgiveness, understanding, acceptance, joy, change, and love. This transition can take years or seconds. The biggest gift I created from this experience is that I was not being punished by experiencing sexual assault; I was being prepared!

Four

GOD KNOWS WHAT HE'S DOING

DUE TO the sexual abuse that began for me at such a young age and the continued sexual activity in my life, I saw sex as natural as breathing. It wasn't a big deal. Because of all the drinking, the partying, and my need to get love and attention, I had sex often.

My mom put me on the pill in fifth grade. We thought that was the best approach because of my activity, but the problem was that I would forget a pill, or take two, only adding to the risk of pregnancy. And of course, it didn't offer any protection from STDs. I wasn't safe from either situation.

I was barely a teen when I got pregnant the first time, and abortion seemed like my only real option. After all, I was so young—how could I take care of another life? So I made that choice a few times, each time adding guilt and shame. Most of all, I felt that it made me a terrible person—a sinner, a murderer. It left me empty inside.

Then, a couple of years later, when I was sixteen, I was dating a guy ten years older than I was. Despite being on the pill, I got pregnant, but I didn't know I was pregnant, due to having my cycle regularly, no sickness, no weight gain, no changes. Nothing was different.

It was Halloween night and I was drinking Everclear, which I had been drinking for about three years almost every weekend. I drank an awful lot, and before this particular Halloween, I had never thrown up from drinking. In fact, not once had I ever gotten sick from it. But that night, I threw up, threw up, and threw up some more. I felt awful. I had never felt so out as I did that night.

The next morning I went to the doctor and said, "I threw up last night and am afraid I'm really sick or something. Maybe I have the flu or a stomach bug."

"Did you drink last night?" she asked. "After all, it was Halloween. Any partying?"

"Yes, but you don't understand. I never get sick."

"Maybe you are pregnant," she responded.

"No! Not possible. We use protection. And I'm having regular periods. I'm good." I was clear.

"Well, let's take the test just to be on the safe side."

I Love Me Not . . .

The test was positive. Yet this time, I didn't have the same reaction as when this had happened before. I was shocked, yet I had a knowing in my heart this time was different. I knew that this baby was special.

"Oh, well, okay."

She did a vaginal exam.

"You're probably about six or seven weeks along."

I went home and slept the whole weekend, trying to avoid my family in the process.

The following week, on Friday night, I was supposed to be at a football game but instead was asleep at home. The next morning, I decided to go to my mom's floral shop and tell her I was pregnant.

I told her, and through her tears and disappointment and grief she said, "All right, we will take care of it. I'll protect you, Kimbo."

I answered, "No, Momma. For whatever reason, this time I am not doing it."

She said, "No, that's not an option. You are going to be someone, Kimberly. You're not throwing away your future! You'll regret this."

But I stood firm in my decision, secure in my knowing and terrified.

We got into a terrible, violent fight. Lots of screaming and yelling and throwing things. Out of sheer desperation, my mom hit me. I was bigger than she was and I grabbed her hands and said, "We are never going to do this again. Are we clear on this?"

In that moment, we knew. This time it was different. Things had changed. She was no longer fighting me; she was helping me. The next day she told my stepfather the news.

I Love Me Not . . .

The next Monday I went to school and then afterward I went to my mom's store. I told her my plans. I had decided I would go live with my friend Janet, who lived two hours away. I was going to do this on my own.

But my mom had her own plan, and she got right to the point. My stepdad had told her, "She can't stay here if she is having that baby. Either she goes or all of you go. She is not going to ruin this family!"

Now, as a mother myself, I feel for my mom. I know it was hard for her because of the choices I had made. I know she made the right decision. But at the time, because of the victim mentality I had, I saw it only one way: *She loved the other kids more than she loved me. I am bad and evil, so she shipped me off, thirteen hours removed from any familiar human connection.* In my mind, I totally deserved to be outcast and alone, at least that was what I heard through my child ears.

My plan had been to go live with my friend, but in the meantime my mom had found the Volunteers of America Maternity Home in New Orleans and called them. My mother had been adopted through VOA of New Orleans, and because of that connection, they accepted me.

Everything was happening too fast. I found out I was pregnant the day after Halloween. Early November I had my birthday, and by Thanksgiving I had moved to New Orleans.

I remember it very clearly. My mom found a safe place for me to go and have my baby. She dropped me off and reminded me that she believed in me. She said, "You'll figure this out. I know you will."

I was so scared and confused. It was fine when it was my plan to leave, yet when she drove away, nothing in my world was fine; the world I knew ended and I was stepping into another life filled with nothing but doubt and fear.

I Love Me Not . . .

The VOA home was no cakewalk. It was hard. Each weekend, I was told that I should love my baby enough to give him up for adoption. But unlike others, I was keeping my baby. The place was full of unwed mothers, all teenagers. Many of the girls would get to go back to their families after they gave birth, but not me. My family had dropped me off to start a new life.

There I was all alone in a new state, a single kid, soon to be a single mom, trying my best to complete school. And par for the course, I met a guy! This guy was different. He was in pain, just like me. We came together to heal and grow, which we did daily.

His name was Kevin. Like me, he had some stuff going on with his family. He kept asking me out and I kept pushing him away, but eventually I gave in and we went to tea. I told him I was pregnant. I gave him my whole life story and told him how my life was changed forever and he said, "Don't worry. We will figure it out." Then he kissed me on my forehead.

"We."

We got together. I stayed home and Kevin went to work. He was nineteen and I was seventeen when we got married. I stayed home with my son, and Kevin worked at a local hotel. He made just five hundred dollars a month, so we lived off welfare and had low-income housing. We were broke, and we were grateful for everything.

The night we got married, I got pregnant with my daughter. Kevin was headed to the Marine Corps and I ended up having my daughter while he was in boot camp. Talk about feeling alone!

There I was, nineteen years old with two kids and I was basically on my own. I was a failure. I didn't even graduate high school. I was validating the definition of white trash and evil that so many had put upon me.

I was raising the little ones on my own for the most part. I was home with them all the time. I felt sorry for them. The negative thoughts would come: *They don't have a chance with me for a mom.* It wasn't just that I didn't know how to function as a healthy mom or how to take care of them; it was that I was growing up with them.

I was a reactive mom. The book I read on how to parent said to spank, so I did. Many times my deep anger surfaced and added to the spankings, many of which they didn't deserve. I yelled from daylight to dark. I didn't know how to do the mom thing. I even had to call home to find out how to heat a baby bottle.

I saw myself as a lost cause, hopeless, alone, and full of hate. I was resentful, ugly, fat, bitter, and dangerous to these babies and anyone else who loved me.

I Love Me . . .

Yet there was a flip side.

I was a young mom. I had tons of energy and took my kids everywhere with me.

I had two babies before I was twenty and can honestly say I wanted both of them then and now. Money was so tight that we qualified for state assistance, which allowed us to have a clean and safe place to live. We never went hungry. I remember walking to the grocery store with my son in his stroller and finding enough change along the way to buy formula. Through the friends we made and the support we had from teachers and peers, we had an old car to drive, a hundred-year-old bed to sleep in, and a reason to get up in the morning.

I wasn't a good momma in the practical sense, but my babies were loved with all I knew how to give. They were good babies and little ones and for the most part very healthy. I thanked God for them every day. I would say, "God, I wasn't good, but they are, and I need help to keep them that way."

Fact = Meaning—the Moment of Shift

When I look back, I realize that those experiences were preparing me for my life that lay ahead. I had so much to get done and so many experiences to have that no matter who stands in front of me or who I am around, I have some level of life experience to use to connect with them.

That is my gift: being prepared.

I know what it is like to have nothing and want everything for my family. I had to figure out how to survive. I thought I was weak because I was emotional and tired, but looking at it now, I recognize that it stretched me so I had room to grow.

I was processing the facts and meanings around being a teen mom. I felt like a failure in society's eyes, yet I was so happy and committed to having my kids. It was like living a good life with an ugly lie attached to it. My children weren't easy or conventional, yet they were mine and I loved them deeply. They taught me so many lessons early in life. God used them to help me become a thriver rather than merely a survivor. He knew I wouldn't slow down the drinking on my own, wouldn't honor my body on my own, wouldn't stop contemplating suicide because of my self-loathing on my own, but that I would do all that and more for my kids.

Two different sides of the same event: the victim side and the responsible side. At sixteen years of age, being a mom was the hardest thing I could ever imagine, but it was truly one of the biggest gifts I have ever received. It seemed lonely and burdensome then, but now I see that my circumstances were actually propelling me toward my goals and dreams.

The fact was that I had two children as a teenage mother.

The meaning I believed then was that I deserved to have my life taken away because I was such a bad person. *Everyone has sex, but I am the slut who deserved to get caught. I have to deal with it.*

One night I learned that truth is truth only because I believe it and I could use the one I had or make up one that served me. I journaled and created a seemingly "crazy" new story. I wrote something similar to the following:

> *I was a gifted child, one who learned daily that being strong was a talent needed to survive. I was becoming so efficient at applying armor that rarely did any part of me see the light of day. Death was a wish my flesh had often, yet I was meant to do significant things for the hearts and minds of millions. Therefore, God brought life into death, light into darkness, love into hate and gave me two babies to love and be loved by. They didn't judge; they only saw goodness, even in my rage. They saved my life. I have been blessed to be a parental figure in the lives of seven children I have called my own. Each one I have hurt, each one I have abandoned on some level, each one I have disrespected with my words and actions, yet I know that each of them knows I have loved them. They taught me what real love is. God wasn't punishing me by giving me two kids by the time I was nineteen; he was teaching me about a special type of love that wasn't limited by blood, authority, or judgment.*
>
> *Today I have loved thousands of people, and my seven angels prepared me for that.*

Which story is true? I made a decision to have faith and believe that the new story could be true, and with commitment and diligence it has become my greatest truth.

A NOTE TO YOU:

My son came to me at a time that I was facing two paths. One ended in death and the other in life. I personally want to thank Kevin for being an angel in my life who understood my pain, my kind of crazy, and loved me anyway.

Jonathon and Lacey, you were the first set of angels God gave to me on this earth. I apologize for the pain I caused you and I am grateful for all the joy you have given me. I would never go back and change a thing about having you in my life when I did. You both have helped me step into my new stories, my new truths, through your love and forgiveness.

James, Courtney, Zach, Sammie, and Timber, I want each of you to hear my heart as I apologize for all the pain I caused you. I love each of you in a special way and thank each of you for teaching me love. I am forever grateful.

Courtney, Zachary, and Sammie, you may not have been my own blood, yet you are three blessings God has used to teach me about love, acceptance, collaboration, and forgiveness. Each of you has a special place in my heart.

James and Timber, God taught me what dessert was when he gave me the two of you—the sweet, beautiful, rich, and yummy part of the meal I call my life. Thank you for always satisfying my sweet tooth with your hearts.

Thank you to the angels that come into our lives for reasons or seasons. In flesh or simply in spirit (as with the babies who didn't come to term), we are better because of you.

Five

ARMOR FOR THE WOUNDED

GROWING UP, I was always in shape and physically attractive by most people's standards. Between ranching and sports, it was not something I put extra effort into; it just came as part of my normal activities. Yet because I flaunted my curves to get attention from anyone who would notice, I opened myself up for people to call me all kinds of ugly names such as whore, trash, and slut. I associated having a beautiful body with manipulation, misunderstanding, and loneliness. My appearance left me feeling unloved, used, and abandoned. It was a mind-set that would lead me down a road of even more pain and suffering in the years to come.

Standing alone in the VOA parking lot, watching as my mother's Suburban pulled away, I stared into the rearview mirror until I could no longer make out my momma's eyes staring back at me. She was leaving me at the home for pregnant teens. I was thirteen hours from home and all alone—well, not completely. I was carrying a little angel who was a savior in my life on many levels.

As I stood there with my hand on my strong and flat tummy, I realized that I would never be alone again. In that moment, the most comforting thought came to my mind: *Since I will always have someone, now I don't have to get a man!* Which also meant I never had to worry about my physical appearance again.

At that time, I was in the most physically satisfying, beautiful shape of my life. I was the strongest I'd ever been, wearing a size six on my five-foot-eight frame of sheer muscle. I was in the prime of my physical life up to that point, but I didn't have to maintain it anymore. *Now I'm going to have someone in my life who is always going to love me and need me,* I thought.

That day, in that moment, I made a decision to let go of my physical prison. After all, on some level "it" was the cause for the abuse I had suffered. I was having a child no one could take away, who would love me not for what I looked like, not for having sex, not for my physical attributes—none of that. My child would love me because that is what a mother and child do. I was his mommy, and that position was something no one could take away from me.

I Love Me Not . . .

Over the next three months, I proceeded to gain ninety pounds—yes, ninety! Between Southern cooking and sheer neglect, it was pretty easy. But the process of gaining so much weight in so little time caused life-threatening physical problems for my pregnancy. I had high blood pressure, toxemia, preeclampsia, diabetes, and stretch marks from head to toe. My breasts, arms, torso, belly, legs—even all the way around my calves—were being pulled apart. My life had a way of doing that (stretching, tearing, and scarring) on so many levels: mental, emotional, and spiritual.

I would literally sit and eat whole large pizzas, blaming it on the fact that I was pregnant. When I got to a size twenty-four, it dawned on me that I was really eating to build and expand my walls of defense. Now my life was complete because of my baby and I no longer needed anyone else in my life.

I believed gaining weight would keep people away. This way, no one would ever try to hit on me and act as if he liked me only to get what he wanted and leave. No one could ever love me. Nobody would ever want anything to do with someone who looked fat, sloppy, and ugly. At least, that's what I thought.

I was proven wrong when Kevin came into my life. I truly believe that he saved me from myself, when I didn't deserve it. Everything about Kevin—everything about our relationship—went against my theory that "no one would love me if I were heavy." My conviction, because of my past, that men wanted me for only my body and sex was proven false. For Kevin that wasn't true at all. In fact, Kevin was a true gentleman, respectful and open. I was closer to him than to anyone I had ever known. He connected with me in so many ways that my physical appearance did not play a primary role in our relationship. He would tell me all the time how beautiful my face was and how much he loved me. He would tell me how smart and amazing I was. He adored me.

For Kevin, it was never about the size of my body, so I responded to that by creating pain where there was none. I told myself, *Oh, great! Kevin accepts me as heavy. It just proves I'm not meant to be happy. I* can have true love only when I am unhealthy [fat], broken [depressed], and ugly [self-hatred].

I Love Me Not . . .

The meaning I chose from this experience was that now that I had my son and Kevin, now that I was heavy, there was no way men could hurt me. No longer would I be the object of others' jealousy for being thin, attractive, and physically fit. No longer would women hate me for the attention I received from men. No one would judge me as a slut or white trash. Being thin and attractive meant being usable, so being fat meant being safe. It meant being loved and trusted by others because I was no longer a threat to them. The fat girl is safe and dispensable.

I didn't have to worry about any of that anymore. My weight was my shield—my defense—that I carried around with me all day long. So I was totally okay with having sleep apnea, high blood pressure, toxemia, and preeclampsia when I was pregnant. I was perfectly fine with wearing a size twenty-four and just sitting around and eating all day. It was worth it because it meant I was safe. For the first time in my life I felt safe!

But then I would look at myself in the mirror and say, "Oh, God, I'm hideous!" In those moments, the frightening image of what I had become was an awful truth to face. It was an ever-growing duality in my life, causing internal conflict, confusion, and despair.

I Love Me . . .

When I realized what was happening, I put the brakes on and said, "Wait a minute!" It really wasn't about what I was eating or how many calories I was taking in; it was the psychological process that occurred when I put on the old meaning and couldn't control my response to it.

Since that time, my health has improved as well as regressed. Through many years on this journey, from medical support by medical doctors to all-natural support by naturopaths, I have lost weight, only to gain more during the next emotional roller coaster. It wasn't until I learned about competing commitments that I learned what my extra weight was really about. It wasn't about the food; it was about my internal belief systems. I discovered I used food as I had used sex, alcohol, and drugs. A great example took place in an Advanced Leadership Seminar. During an exercise, a female student commented, "You would never understand, Kimberly. You don't know what it's like to struggle with weight. You've probably always been beautiful. You're one of those skinny, rich snobs we all hate." I just laughed in that moment. *If only you knew the truth,* I thought. Yet later I replayed that statement over and over again in my mind. All of a sudden I was hungry and craving wine, candy, and fried food. Within a month, I had gained thirteen pounds.

Fact = Meaning—the Moment of Shift

Looking back on the years that I forfeited to obesity and poor health since the age of seventeen, I'm not angry; I am grateful. The good Lord must have given me the health points of ten people, because each time my body is tested, it keeps surviving. No one understands how, yet it does. (Thanks, God.)

So I chose to go from a woman who had to stay fat to stay safe, invisible, and unlovable, to a healthy woman who has great curves, can play on the field of life with professional and successful athletes, and surrounds herself with secure, grounded, and healthy people who value her light and demand that it grows.

Today I work with men, women, and teens who look at my five-foot-eight 145-pound frame and assume I have no idea how they feel. They can't imagine that someone they see as pretty or having an average build once referred to her clothes as tent size. Releasing more than a hundred pounds completely startles people and alters their view of you.

Every time I shower and shave my legs, I see the hundreds of stretch marks that remind me of the embarrassment, blame, disgust, and guilt I endured for more than fifteen years. I know the looks that are cast on obese and unhealthy people. I know the shame of not respecting my body and, even worse, the feeling of helplessness to change it. I understand the desire to give up on every part of me—the mental, emotional, spiritual, and physical. Today I see every moment as a gift, and here's why.

I know that when I'm living a life of self-love and self-compassion, I can have a healthy body. I know that my body is an integral part of who I am and that my spirit can't keep going forward if my body is not in alignment. I know that the only way I can live the life I want to lead is to treat my body with the care and respect it deserves.

I understand that I can control what I put in my mouth, yet without doing the healing developmental work on my negative beliefs, I can't have a healthy outside with a toxic inside. The thoughts that go through my heart and head have a direct contribution to what my exterior looks like. I also know now that I have a choice every moment of every day. That's how much power I have and that's how much power you have.

A NOTE TO YOU:

A favorite quote that my husband, Tim, reminds me of daily is "All disappointment is the result of an unfavorable comparison." At forty-two years old, I am just now developing a clue about what that means. I have been exposed to beautiful people who have millions of dollars and unlimited resources, as well as beautiful people with little more than a couple of bags to hold all their belongings, with the world's resources (sun, wind, rain) at their fingertips.

I have coached women and men with exterior perfection unmatched by millions and have coached men and women with content, context, and talent that you would never even notice if you hadn't tripped over these individuals in the street. I am learning that true beauty—our growth, grace, mistakes, and how we own them—is in our hearts. True beauty shows up in our vulnerability, our humanity, and our faults. Beauty appears in the scars that are seen and unseen on the bodies and souls of the people who are getting back up after they fall. It's not in the size four perfect build or the thirty-two-inch waist. It's not the perfect build or perfect boobs.

Beauty is my mess-ups that I learn from and apologize for. It's for my ah-ha's and applications. It's my trusting too much and being betrayed. It's life's hurts and blessings. The physical body is my opportunity to challenge, honor, and strengthen the exterior vehicle on my journey.

OLD

FACT		MEANING
BODY OVERWEIGHT	=	SAFETY
THIN BODY	=	ABUSE/NEGLECT
PEOPLE SAW ME AS FAT	=	I AM LESS THAN THEM

NEW

FACT		MEANING
BODY OVERWEIGHT	=	UNRESOLVED ISSUES
THIN BODY	=	RESPECT FOR EXTERIOR VEHICLES
PEOPLE SAW ME AS FAT	=	AN OUTWARD CRY FOR INWARD SUPPORT

Six

A PRISON OF MY OWN MAKING

I WAS seventeen years old when I married Kevin. He was my first love and showed me kindness, love, and acceptance in a way I had never received from a man before. He saw *me*—not as an object or someone to use or something to possess, but as a person. He was gracious and supportive and always encouraged me to take chances, plan for more, and dream.

At the time we met, we both needed someone, so the choice seemed obvious. I was all alone, scared, and about to become a mother. He was searching for his purpose in life and had a need to be accepted for who he was. He had huge aspirations but wasn't sure how to go about making them a reality. So, for that season in our lives, we were exactly what the other person needed. We were just too young and naive to realize that the foundation we were building on wasn't likely to withstand the "life" that lay ahead of us.

Kevin was my best friend and taught me that I could be loved for who I was, yet we married in order to survive. I loved him more than I had loved anyone at that point, but I was never *in* love with him, nor he with me. Not really! I do believe we thought we were then. I do believe we loved each other as much as two wounded, scared, abandoned, and lost souls could when barely starting out in life. We were connected in a weird, multi-life kind of way, more brother and sister than passionate lovers.

We respected each other and cared for the overall well-being of the other, yet the husband/wife story line wasn't flowing and we both wondered if we were doing it wrong. Were we missing something?

After being totally honest with each other, we decided there really ought to be more to a marriage and we weren't going to be able to meet that need for each other. In the end, we decided to let go, each in our own way. Kevin and I decided to end "us" so that we could find what each of us needed. We both were ready to begin again. Little did I know that I was about to walk down an old, familiar path. I gave away my chance at having a safe, predictable, and normal life, only to replace it with a situation that resurrected all of the deep-seated insecurities and torment of my youth.

I Love Me Not . . .

After Kevin and I went our separate ways, it wasn't long before I started hitting the country bars. I loved to line-dance, and I was dancing when I met Eric. For me, the attraction was immediate. He was the classic charming and mischievous type—the life of the party. He was a "good-time guy" who was emotionally unavailable. The more distant he was, the more I wanted him. I pursued him for several months.

At this point in my life, I was divorced, had two kids, and was working for an insurance company. In many ways, it seemed that I had my life together. But old patterns and behaviors from my past began to resurface.

Eric was a master manipulator. He would play games with me—giving me attention sometimes, only to withhold it later. I knew this game! And because my identity was deeply rooted in this sort of behavior, it worked. I was a mental and emotional prisoner.

I would do anything for Eric, and the closer I got to him, the more I became aware of how broken he was, which only attracted me more. He had alcoholic parents and no real relationship with his family. Everything in his life—his prior relationships, his past, everything he had been through—was unfair (according to him). The guys at work got paid more money even though he always did more work. He deserved a promotion, yet someone else always got it. Life wasn't fair. Love wasn't fair.

Eric had a dark side that was deep and lonely. He had a frantic, lost-child feel about him that invited the misguided, naive healer inside me. All the while, I saw glimpses of destruction within him that I felt I was supposed to stop or change somehow. Eric was a master of illusion. He gave most of the good people in my life an uneasy feeling, yet he would lure all of them into the web of stories and events he had spun, and it seemed as though no one ever escaped.

Sadly, the more alienating Eric became, the more I was insistent on loving him and saving him from himself. *I'll show him,* I thought. *I can fix this. I'll prove to him that love can be good. It can be healing, safe, different with me.*

So we dated. It was rocky at best, yet both of us were sick enough to stick it out. Heck, we'd even have fun. We loved to dance together and laugh at each other; we played risky games, smoked, and drank a lot. We had an adventurous sex life and did all the things carefree young adults do. Our mission was F.U.N.—whatever that looked like in the moment. After all, I had essentially missed my whole adolescence. I knew he was broken, but so was I. I thought we were on the same playing field—until the day we got married.

I Love Me Not...

We were married in Tennessee. We had the picture-perfect fall mountain wedding. Our families attended and all seemed perfect. I was really looking forward to our honeymoon. That night Eric got in bed and turned away from me. I reached out to touch him and he snapped, "Get away from me!" He physically recoiled from me.

"What!" I exclaimed. "What is wrong with you?"

"You are nasty. Get away from me," he said. "Go take a shower."

I was confused. I reacted sharply and cursed.

He said, "You will never talk like that again. You are dirty. Go take a shower."

Over the next few weeks, Eric went from being the outgoing life of the party to a dominating, closed-off, hateful tyrant. I had known he was broken before I married him, but he had always been reachable. Now he completely shut me down and out.

It was as though Eric put me on a shelf—like some kind of memorabilia—and when he went out, he dated other people. Eric was in the military, and every time he went out on deployment, he would have a new girlfriend, plus several "friends with benefits." I would catch him and he would lie. He would yell and scream without even stopping to breathe. He turned things around with such fierceness that I would give in and admit to things I didn't even do just to get him to stop, and he would clamp down on me even harder.

It all happened so quickly that I was literally in shock for months. I wasn't allowed to smoke, cuss, or drink, and absolutely no sex. But he could—behind my back, in my own home, with other women. He just didn't want to have sex with me.

I would beg and plead for his attention and he would usually say no. If I could get him in a good enough mood to have sex, he would say I did it all wrong. I needed to shower because I smelled bad, even after I'd showered just an hour earlier. I was supposedly dirty and gross, for no other reason than just because I was. On and on it went, and it got to the point that I couldn't wait for him to be gone during the day or on deployment. At least then I could live. It was the only time I could breathe.

Eric was so mean to my children. He would swat them and punish them military style by having them lean against the wall in a squatting position for thirty to forty-five minutes. Push-ups and sit-ups in the hundreds were standard. They would scream and cry, and as soon as Eric got them scared enough to not yell anymore, he would quit. Every time I would try to intervene, he would threaten me mentally and physically, so I would just sit with them, holding them and helping them to stop crying so it would end. I didn't know what else to do.

I tried to figure out why Eric had changed, why he hated me and anyone I cared about. *Maybe he's trying to prove to me that love won't work—that it isn't true.* I didn't want him to be "right." I had long since realized my divorce from Kevin was a huge mistake. Getting divorced wasn't the answer, and I wasn't going to make the same mistake twice. No matter how bad it got, I wasn't quitting, so I pressed in all the more to show him that love can be true. Love stays. Love commits. Love is right.

I tried so hard, but things only got worse. The angrier he was, the more he drank and the more he physically pushed and hit me and my kids. I would say to him, "You're scaring me. I don't like this!" He answered by telling me that the only way I would leave our marriage was in a body bag and that if I didn't straighten up, my kids would pay too.

Eric got stationed in Japan, and of course I followed him. At this point, our relationship was so toxic that I wasn't sure which I was more terrified of: staying with him and putting up with his insane drinking and physical abuse, or learning how to live life again after having been a mental and physical prisoner. I had a crazy fear of not living in the hyper-structure Eric demanded.

I went overseas with the hope that a new start would fix everything and maybe even be the very change we needed. Instead, my life was on a downward spiral that I had no idea how to stop.

We lived in military housing, and as luck would have it, the backyards of the houses backed up to each other. We were blessed because our house was one of the few that had a large back patio. I became friends with my neighbors, and when Eric was away, we would meet on my back porch for coffee every morning. Our preschool-aged kids would play together during the day and we often shared meals together, including dinners with their entire families. These friends were the main exposure to family and kindness that my children and I experienced while living overseas.

When Eric came home, he made me lock the back door. We weren't allowed to go onto the back porch, and my friends weren't allowed to come over. They weren't allowed in the house because he didn't like them; he thought they were trash. But as soon as he would leave, everyone would begin gathering at my house again. He was angry because he wanted to control me and the neighbors, and he couldn't while he was gone. But he made us pay.

Another irrational demand Eric had was that I wasn't allowed to speak to any of his commanding officers or their wives when we attended military social events. He expected me to volunteer and make him look good. Yet if he ever saw me talking to anyone of importance, I would get scolded and interrogated when we got home. He would yell, scream, and push me around, all because he was terrified I would tell them what was really going on at home. The saddest part was he didn't need to worry, as I wouldn't have said anything because it was too embarrassing and humiliating for me to admit.

Eric began drinking all the time. He would go out with his buddies and I would hide the kids to protect them; sometimes I would have them sleep under their beds so they were out of sight. I had to make sure everything was perfect, as Eric's OCD was extreme when he drank. Dinner had to be ready when he came home, even if it were two in the morning. The house had to be kept a certain way, and the kids had to behave a certain way. If not, the price was high.

We weren't allowed even the simplest pleasure or fun when he was around. The abuse was so bad that I ended up in the hospital multiple times with a broken cheekbone, bruises, and cuts. Yet I kept trying. I stayed with him; after all, I was sure I could save him.

Nobody understood why I stayed. I honestly didn't understand it either, with the years of being tested and falling short and paying the piper. I was trained to be scared by a look or a breath. I knew how bad the night would be just based on the volume of his voice. I was living in a mental, physical, and emotional prison. It was hell every day that Eric was around, yet I knew this hell. I thought things were hard with Kevin and I quit. What if I quit again and it only got worse? I worried I'd die.

I was desperate for attention and companionship. When Eric was gone, I would go out to the bars just looking for attention, and if that meant I came home with someone, that was fine with me. I just wanted someone to be nice to me. Of course, the whole time I was terrified that if I got caught, Eric would kill me.

I was emotionally numb after years of being ignored and resented. I'm not proud of the fact that I sought love in the countless faces of other lost souls. I was so deep in anger, revenge, hate, fear, and unforgiveness that I was a toxic, broken, and lost wife and mother. I completely justified my unfaithful behavior by pinning it all on Eric: *If he had done this, then I wouldn't have done that.* More lies. One thing I knew for sure was that if Eric ever caught me cheating, he would kill me. Some days I was careless, hoping he would notice and life would end—I believed ending my prison sentence would be a gift.

One day Eric came home and jumped up and sat on the countertop. This was not like him at all; everything had to be perfect, especially when it came to decorum and manners. But there he was perched above me and looking down at me. "Being married isn't as much fun as I thought it would be. I want a divorce," he said, his voice sounding like that of a thirteen-year-old boy.

I looked at him, and my first thought was that he was going to hurt me. Apparently, he had done drugs or something, because he seemed crazy. Something had to be wrong. *He's going to do something to me or the kids!* My mind was racing.

After his announcement, he jumped down from the counter, again with a jovial disposition.

"Are you feeling okay?" I asked. "I know you've been working nights."

He responded, "This is my decision—enough!" Short and to the point.

That was the last thing he said about it, and we went back to life as usual. I kept up my routine of trying to be good enough, worthy enough, careful enough. Keeping house and cooking his favorite meals. Taking care of my kids, working, and paying the bills.

He never said another word about divorce until one night months later. I let my guard down for a few hours. We were talking and listening to each other. When I had done everything I was supposed to do—showered and scrubbed perfectly clean—we had sex. *Finally,* I thought, *we are normal again.* Granted, it happened only a couple of times a year.

Then the next morning I said, "We need to think about our plans for Christmas. Are we staying here or going home?"

"Christmas?" he said, laughing. "You're gonna be long gone before then."

I thought he was having one of his fits. But he said it again. "We will be divorced by then."

Without even breathing, I responded with "okay." I knew he was serious. I had seen the look of finality on his face. *What do I do?*

I Love Me . . .

Over the next couple of weeks, I felt out of sorts even more than usual. I missed my period. I knew something was wrong. Sure enough, the pregnancy test was positive. I panicked. *Now what am I going to do?* I threw away the testing-kit supplies. I didn't want him to find out until I had a plan.

The moment I realized I was pregnant, it dawned on me that if I brought another baby into this world, he could very well kill me and my two kids just so he could have *his* kid all to himself. Eric had always said that he would never divorce me, as Catholics don't get divorced and he wasn't going to get in trouble with God because of me. So when he began talking about divorce, I interpreted that to mean that my life was in very real danger, because in his eyes, death (mine) was the only way out, and this would be especially true with our child playing into the mix.

It became obvious to me that there were two very real options: either I could tell Eric I was pregnant and he would go along with this pregnancy to get *his* baby and something would mysteriously happen to me and my older kids, or I could run now. I could ask for help and escape his grip, and that is exactly what I did.

It was the very real fear for my life and the lives of my children that drove me to take a chance and ask for help.

The very next day, I went to the hangar and talked to Eric's commanding officer. I laid everything out for him: all my medical records, reports from neighbors, all the photos. Fortunately, he took the situation seriously. He believed me, and he stood up for me and protected me. We had many things we had to do legally, but he said he would make it happen and would arrange for me and my kids to be off the island safely in less than a few days. And he did exactly what he'd promised.

Before ten days had passed, I was back home in Texas with two little ones, two puppies, and a healthy baby boy on the way.

Fact = Meaning—the Moment of Shift

The fact was I allowed a man to drink heavily and beat me on a regular basis. I made it mean that I must be a terrible, evil, bad girl who believed everything Eric said, so I deserved to be hit, yelled at, and controlled. I felt like a caged animal, yet I truly believed I was so bad that I needed Eric to help keep me contained. The moment of shift occurred when I sat down on the couch in our living room. I put my hands on my belly and said out loud, "God, I can't allow Eric to get his hands on this baby." It dawned on me that God gave me this baby so I could muster the strength to leave. He gave me this baby to wake me up and get me out of this situation. God knew I didn't see myself as worthy enough to get out, but for the kids I would. Then I realized that I really couldn't be evil if God gave me one of his angels.

I got away from Eric and am forever grateful. I escaped. I went home. And Eric went on with his life. He beat his second wife so severely she lost hearing in one ear. His third wife was beaten so badly she suffered permanent brain damage.

I escaped. Thank God.

A NOTE TO YOU:

Looking back, it is obvious that I got out in the nick of time. It was a trying and frightening experience, but I learned that I will never allow another human being to determine my worth. I will never again let anyone speak to me the way Eric did. The truth of the matter was that he was speaking to me the same way *I* was speaking to me. Eric never said anything to me that I hadn't already said to myself.

The fear and physical pain were just illusions compared to the power and control Eric had over my mind. He taught me that I teach people how to treat me—that I get to determine what the quality of my life is like.

I realized that truth then and know it even more now. I am very grateful for that experience because it fortified me. It created resilience in me so that no matter how hard I get pushed down by life, I get back up, no matter what.

I suffered through several years of abuse and neglect. I have decided that no one (not even my own negative self-talk) gets to determine who I am, what I am, or what I do. I am an amazing person, but I just had to hit bottom to gain the awareness of that.

Now when things go wrong, hurt, or don't make sense, I get to choose. I have the ability to walk away. I can ask for help, and there are people who will protect me and come to my aid. I always have a choice; I am not a victim. I have stepped into my power—the power that was there all along. The same is true for you.

OLD

FACT		MEANING
OVERWEIGHT	=	DISGUSTING, FAT, SMELLY
VERBALLY ABUSED	=	I DESERVED EVERY WORD AND IT WAS ALL TRUE
PHYSICALLY ABUSED	=	IF I WERE A BETTER PERSON, HE WOULDN'T NEED TO KEEP ME IN LINE

NEW

FACT		MEANING
OVERWEIGHT	=	UNRESOLVED ISSUES
VERBALLY ABUSED	=	WHEN MY INTERNAL TALK CHANGES, SO WILL THAT OF OTHERS
PHYSICALLY ABUSED	=	WHEN I TAKE CARE OF MYSELF, OTHERS WILL TAKE CARE OF ME TOO

Seven

A LITTLE WINE GOES A LONG WAY

I WAS probably ten years old when I started stealing from my momma's liquor stash. Although this seems a bit shocking to some, in many ways it was a logical reaction to my emotional experiences.

My mother was adopted by a well-to-do family in the Houston area. She was exposed to drinking early on, for it was part of the social order. Like so many other behaviors that get passed from one generation to the next, what my mom learned, my siblings and I soon learned as well. When you had a good time, you drank, and when things were bad, you drank. When you were bored, rushed, stressed, angry, or confused, you drank. It was the perfect answer to all of life's situations.

Think about it: the government says it's legal, so it is basically a mind-numbing substance that has been "popularized" and approved by society. If a little works a little, then a lot will work even better. Makes sense. You can look cool, feel nothing, and start applying this substance at 6:00 a.m. with a Bloody Mary. Alcohol easily crosses social situations. It connects the unconnected. It always seems like an easy way into and out of everything.

As a young child, with all of the sexual stuff, insecurities, and abandonment issues, I felt very out of control. I was determined not to let anyone else hurt me, so the need to control everything ruled my life. I became very inflexible, dominant, and hard. It was impossible to please me, and I was often unfriendly and unkind. It was my armor.

The truth is, I walked through life panicked on a daily basis. I worried that I couldn't earn my momma's love by being useful enough. I worried that someone would find out about the dark side going on sexually. I worried that the money I stole from my stepdad weekly would stop, and then how would I buy my friendships? I worried that the Hispanic girls who hated me would actually find me and beat my white ass. I worried my stepdad would get rid of me every time I messed up. I worried that I would get fat and no boys would want to be with me. I worried about everything and everyone—all of this by the time I was just ten years old.

I became a royal brat. I acted like the trapped animal that I was. Even the people who had nothing but kindness and good intentions got harmed while interacting with me. My siblings and family suffered my rage. And just beneath the surface, at all times, my anger only grew.

The problem was that I didn't know how to let go, enjoy, or allow anything to just be. I had no idea how to loosen up without help from a bottle. It was my escape for a while. After all, I could actually have some downtime once I reached the level of intoxication that shut down the death grip I had on life. Because I was so young, a lot of my drinking happened alone. Once I reached junior high, I started hanging out with high schoolers, and drinking seemed normal at that level.

Drinking was exciting, it was easier than reality, it helped numb all the voices, but it was a double-edged sword. When my parents, their friends, or other relatives drank, it was always in an extreme fashion. They never just went home to have *a* nice glass of wine. No, they drank when they partied, they drank when they had friends over, they drank socially, they drank alone—extremes were always involved. I kept this toxic lifestyle going for myself and my children.

If my mom and stepdad drank and everything was going well and they were happy, they were very loving people and I was the best kid in the world. Even my stepdad—who didn't like me all that much back then—loved me to death when he was drinking. But if anything went wrong, things got really bad. There were vicious fights, rages, throwing things. I watched my mom get hurt and my family be destroyed by words, threats, and actions that could never be taken back or forgotten. But, sadly, I followed that pattern as well.

I Love Me Not . . .

By the time I was twelve, I was already five-foot-eight, 145 pounds, and wearing a size 38 bra. Needless to say, I had developed very early. I was driving and I totally looked the part, so I was the one who could go and get alcohol for myself, my friends, and everyone I wanted to like me.

They didn't check ID as carefully back then like they do now, so I could buy it and give it away to my friends. I was happy to help anybody; I was the "get it" girl. I was stealing money each week from my stepdad to buy alcohol for anyone who wanted it. Yes, I wanted them to be my friends, to like me, but mainly I drank to not care, and doing it with others made it seem a little more acceptable, a little more normal, just a little better.

Around age thirteen, I discovered something new that worked in half the time, every time: Everclear. Often, sometimes daily, I would go buy a pint of Everclear and pour the whole thing into a Route 44 slush. I would stir it around and gulp it down, and in about thirty to forty-five minutes, I would be drunker than Cooter Brown. The buzz would last as long as I needed it to, and I would laugh and have a good time.

I am going to repeat that last statement: I would laugh and have a good time. I had never allowed myself to develop a laugh; I had never learned fun. I was never able to step into "her"—the girl who could—without an outside substance. I longed for that other side of me: the light side, the courageous side. My only access to it seemed through this door. *The emergency exit.*

Sadly, the next day I would go back and do it all over again. I would do anything to have it back. I drank more and more, but it never seemed to be enough to keep me in a place of connection with myself or others for long.

At fourteen I had a fake ID and was going to dances all over South Texas. I would get all dressed up and start preflighting whatever alcohol I could get my hands on. I'd choose the man I would get attention from that night, and the race was on.

I hung out with a much older crowd and would go into the twenty-one-and-over clubs in Corpus Christi. I would leave home Wednesday or Thursday and go dancing and wouldn't return home until Sunday or Monday.

Even though my mom fought my behavior, pleaded for different actions, demanded respect, punished me, withheld material things, and begged me to stop, it's what I did. I never once deliberately did anything to hurt her or my family. In the moment, my survival was all I could focus on. I didn't know how to do anything else.

I Love Me Not . . .

I had to be in control because if I weren't, I would get hurt. But I had a love/hate relationship with alcohol. I would watch my mom battle it and how it owned her at times, especially when life got hard. I remember the resentment I had for those situations and then recognizing that I was out doing the same thing.

The morning I found out I was pregnant with my oldest son, I stopped drinking. I moved to Louisiana and eventually married Kevin. We were so poor that we probably didn't drink for several years. I never physically missed drinking. I believed in my mind that having a baby, someone to love and be loved by, saved me. I didn't need the alcohol—at least not for a little while. But soon Kevin joined the military and our marriage was not fulfilling our individual needs, so we decided to start going out to party on our own. It didn't take long for me to pick up where I left off.

Many years later, I started dating a man living in a nearby city who had been in an Alcoholics Anonymous 12-step recovery program and had twenty years of sobriety. He treated me as if I were normal. He didn't have any issues with my drinking, but I realized he had something I didn't have: He had peace of mind in his life, whether things were easy or hard.

One night I'd had a really bad night of drinking and felt horrible. The next morning, I was in the bathtub and shared with P. J., "I don't drink really often, but I'm drinking for the wrong reasons. I'm drinking so I don't have to feel pain. I'm drinking so I can let go of control. I'm drinking so I don't have to pay attention to life. I'm drinking so I can feel anything good."

It was a true wake-up call for me. Even if it was just once a month, I was drinking only to relieve some kind of emotional stressor. I was drinking for all the wrong reasons. So that night—it was September 9—I went to my first meeting of Alcoholics Anonymous.

I didn't drink another drop for ten years.

During that time, I had to face many situations and deal with feelings that in the past I had always numbed with alcohol. I would go to family functions and have relatives or friends mock me and call me ugly names. Before, when they treated me that way, I would have a drink and I didn't care. I became deaf to their words. But once I was sober, I could hear all of it. I had to face the consequences of having cheated on my husbands, face the people I had stolen money from and those I was mean to. It was the first time since I was a little kid that I did not have something to help me cope. It was hard, raw, and very painful.

I Love Me . . .

During those ten years, I walked through the twelve steps eight different times. I did all of my character development work with Klemmer & Associates and literally dozens of other programs. I started working on the insecurities, dysfunction, inadequacies, abuse, neglect, abandonment, issues with my father, issues with my mother—all of the reasons I was in this position in the first place.

My family and close friends disagreed with my choice to go to AA. They didn't believe I had a problem, yet I knew I wanted to be numb and would do what it took when things got bad enough. I knew the possibility was there. I chose not to drink for ten years, and with my dad's having a severe allergy to alcohol and my having been around alcohol my whole life, it just made sense for me. Maybe I wasn't an alcoholic by *their* definition, but I knew I was drinking for all the wrong reasons, and AA helped me see that I needed to take care of me and own all parts of me.

Only in the last few years have I begun having a drink from time to time, safely and accountable to the people whom I have asked to keep me in check. It has been an interesting journey. The last few years there have been a few occasions I have picked up a drink to alter my mood, numb my pain, or avoid my reality, and I'm very aware and conscious of that. It's an alert. It means I have more personal work to do. And I love that today I have the willingness to test my truth: to stop, get help, grow, repeat. I know there are times I am tempted. I am learning to listen to the Holy Spirit within me and consume alcohol only when I am in true choice (making a conscious decision to do so).

Today a glass of wine at dinner or a drink at the end of the day with my husband or close friends does not present a problem. Instead, it's a time to connect and break bread. Years ago I drank to drown out all the things I couldn't control. Today I have realized that living has nothing to do with control and am grateful for learning that through the Heart of the Samurai course offered by Klemmer & Associates.

One of the deepest belief systems I have battled is the illusion of control. Many of the battles I have faced occurred when my life got out of control or it looked like it could. My battles provided a place for many to be injured. At Heart of the Samurai, I learned what surrender is and how it helps me and others. It has forever changed my world.

The key to my being successful and being able to live freely without having to control everything around me is to choose what meaning truly serves my future, my dreams, and my commitments.

Fact = Meaning—the Moment of Shift

The undisputed fact (in my mind) is that from a very young age I would drink to get drunk, I would drink to not feel, I would drink to relax, and I would drink to let go of control. I would drink to simply fit in.

The aha moment in this experience was realizing I was drinking for the wrong reasons. Many unfortunate events that occurred while I was drinking helped motivate me to stop using alcohol in an abusive manner. Ten years away from alcohol gave me time to really be open and honest with myself. Without the distraction, I was able to work on my emotional baggage. Staffing Personal Mastery, Advanced Leadership Seminars, and Heart of the Samurai and coaching Samurai Camp dozens of times over the last thirteen years have helped me get to the core of many of my issues. Today I am so grateful for the support system I had in my life so I could address those needs. I knew that I had to do something differently—that I had to get a hold of my life and peel away the layers of my past with love and support.

A NOTE TO YOU:

Alcoholism is a very personal disease. I believe there are truly people who are suffering from an illness they cannot restrain from. After ten years of intense therapy, emotional support, and having a lot of really good people in my life, I got to a place in which I was considering drinking again. So I sat down with my closest friends and explained the questions I had about what it all meant. I asked for help to work through my sets of sunglasses and earmuffs around my fear of failure, my fear of what others might think, my fear of "What if I'm wrong?"

I have asked to be held to a higher standard, and I request and am open to feedback. I am saddened to say that I have fallen short and allowed my drinking to become about avoidance and numbing myself a few times over the last several years. But I am so blessed because when I have dealt with relationships poorly or used wine to connect with people instead of using my heart, I have the kind of friends who will support me with honesty, feedback, and accountability. Because of my deeper competing commitments and the depth of the emotional and physical abuse I overcame, I will always have to pay attention to slippery situations and be steadfast in continued growth, therapy, support, and the commitment to being a better version of me each day. Funny enough, some days I hit the bull's-eye and other days I believe even God thinks I should get back in bed and stay there for a while.

I want to say, from my heart to yours, that if anything I have shared about my story (abuse, neglect, pain) rings true for you or someone you love, please reach out for help. And please allow time to receive that help! Nothing that lasts is a quick fix. My mentors have all shared that you can't quit something until you have committed fully to it. When you reach out for help, you don't get to quit or refuse it until you have truly received the help every situation has for you. I highly recommend 12-step recovery programs for people who want help. I also would say that using any "excuse" not to step into the best version of you is still just an excuse. Be aware and be real with yourself.

I believe in a higher power today because of the help I got from Alcoholics Anonymous. Today I look at my drinking history as my darkness before the dawn. I have learned and applied and relearned and reapplied over and over again. Please hear my heart when I say that if you have questions, if you wonder, if you know you want something different, get help. You deserve it, and so do all the people who deserve to hear how you overcame so you could help others.

It is an individual situation and only you can make those decisions for yourself. You should never make a decision based on someone else's story, including mine. My advice is that you seek out professional help: a doctor, a counselor, someone who has training in addiction, someone who can give you safe and grounded support.

OLD

FACT	MEANING
DRINKING YOUNG	= MAKES LIFE EASIER
DRINKING TO FEEL	= I WAS WEAK AND NEEDED OUTSIDE INFLUENCES
DRINKING TO CONNECT	= I DON'T UNDERSTAND PEOPLE AND THEY SCARE ME

NEW

FACT	MEANING
DRINKING YOUNG	= NOT EDUCATED OR ASKING FOR HELP
DRINKING TO FEEL	= I HAD TO FEEL HEALTHY EXAMPLES OF OTHER EXPRESSIONS OF SELF
DRINKING TO CONNECT	= I GET TO EXPLORE OTHER MECHANISMS TO CONNECT TO PEOPLE

Eight

I CAN'T REMEMBER WHEN...

I WAS I was in my midtwenties when I got sick. I went to bed Christmas night and woke up the next day in excruciating pain. Every joint in my body throbbed and I couldn't even move. I literally woke up with my major joints and limbs doubled in size.

It was inexplicable. I was completely normal one day, dreadfully sick the next. I was young and in the prime of my life. I had three young kids to chase after and instead found myself confined to a bed most of the day.

I spent the next several months seeing doctors and undergoing tests, looking for answers, but no one could find anything. I started receiving cortisone shots to alleviate some of the pain, but still there were no real answers. Then one day a doctor diagnosed me with an aggressive form of lupus that attacks all connective tissues in the joints, the brain, and many organs.

Lupus. I finally had an answer and began treatment, but the pain still continued. I was in and out of the hospital for months until the point that I was too weak to walk or go anywhere at all. Then, on top of the lupus, I developed a tumor behind my right orbit—an inflammatory tumor that appeared overnight. Once again, the impact was immediate. On Wednesday, my eye hurt and my face was a little swollen. By Friday, the entire area from the base of my hairline to my collar bone was protruding. After two more days, the pain was so intense that I had to be put on a morphine drip. I spent nearly four more weeks in the hospital and was given the prognosis that I had less than a year to live. The grim report got even grimmer.

For a total of nearly two and a half years, I could not physically get around; even walking from my bed to the kitchen was nearly impossible. My youngest child at the time was just three, but I was no longer able to be an active mom. I would do my best to muster what energy I could and participate with my kids to the best of my ability. Then I would sleep for three to four days afterward. So friends and family took care of my kids. After a while, my memory started to fail. The worse the lupus got, the less my memory worked, and the tumor caused me to lose all short-term memory. Obviously, I was in no condition to work, so there was no income. I was supported by my credit cards, friends, and family.

At times, I would manage to get out to the local store and would get so confused that I couldn't find my way home. One time I ended up more than an hour and a half away from home. Thankfully, one of the many times this happened, the police kindly escorted me home. I was listless and felt completely useless. I spent my days waiting to die.

I Love Me Not . . .

I lost so much time in my life: time with my kids, time doing what I wanted to be doing, time doing the everyday, basic things we all take for granted. I was so eager to find an answer, a cure, but after seeing five specialists and undergoing experimental drugs and therapies, it became apparent that doctors could offer me no helpful escape from the hell I called my life. My kids lost out in so many ways; I couldn't take part in their lives the way a healthy mom would. My sickness made me a victim and them, too. I was hopeless, suffering from chronic pain, memory loss, fear, and disappointment. Basically, I quit life. I just wanted it to end—and soon.

Looking back, I realize that at the time, I couldn't see past the pain, the fear, or the unknown. It blinded me to any step that might have been possible. There was nothing I could do. So I became hopeless, dependent, and resentful.

One minute I cried, "Why me?" The next minute I was sure this was my punishment for all the bad things I had done, the lies I told, the times I cheated and stole, the people I hurt. I felt as though I deserved to die, and the faster I died, the better it would be for my kids. After all, they couldn't have a "good" mom; I just didn't have it in me. As morbid as it sounds, I believed that at least a dead mom could not do more harm.

This bad situation couldn't have possibly gotten worse. I didn't have the faith for this. I just wanted to fade into the darkness, for I was certain I deserved nothing else.

I was sexually abused as a child. I had my first baby at sixteen, my second by nineteen. I had been married, divorced, married again to an alcoholic and extremely abusive husband, and divorced again. And now, I was dying of a devastating sickness in my midtwenties. I grew sicker and sicker by the day.

This is because you are bad and evil, Kimberly. This is the penance that you have to pay. God is punishing you. The thoughts were relentless. I lay there trapped in my own hell, contemplating ways I could stop the pain. Every time I hurt someone with my anger and rage—knowingly or unknowingly—I wanted to die at all costs. Time, which should have been a gift, seemed like a prison sentence. My daily goals consisted of hurting less and dying sooner.

The answer to my pain came in a most unexpected way. I climbed up out of that dark pit, mostly to make my mom leave me alone. She just wouldn't stop nagging me to take these nutritional supplements she had heard about. One day she could tell that my pain was extreme and knew I couldn't get up, so she turned on a video that told me about what the products could do, over and over again. I was a captive audience.

I begged my mom to stop. "Momma, please leave me alone. Let me die. I'm so tired." She responded, "Do this last thing, Kimbo, please, and then I will stop." I really didn't care, but she wouldn't let up. So I ordered the supplements that had a money-back guarantee, which was good because if there were no improvement, I would get my money back and the bills would still get paid. The products were all-natural and were a fine, airy, chalky powder with no real taste.

My mom helped me research and we learned the value in taking different doses at different points in the body's healing process. But I came up with a plan that my mom didn't know about. I decided that I would take the maximum amount allowed every day. I had to get through twelve tubs of powder, so I wanted to do it as quickly as possible. Then, when nothing happened, I could get my money back and pay my bills.

Well, in a weird way, my need to be right and prove this was just another waste of time by following their rules, my way, saved my life.

First, the swelling started going down. My need for 120 steroids per day lessened, and my blood pressure began to come down as well. Within a few months, I could walk around my local track and started getting mobile again. But even though physical healing was coming, the loss of my memory was a bitter regret.

I Love Me Not . . .

I'd always had an epic memory—until I lost it. Prior to this illness consuming my existence, I basically had a photographic memory. I was able to seal every detail, track every word spoken, remember every thought. I used this gift to lie, cheat, and steal my way through life. I could spin a story and make anyone listen, all while keeping the details locked up in my brain as though it were a vault and only I held the code.

I used the gift of my exceptional memory to gain leverage, even if that meant hurting others. I used it to make things work in my life but rarely used it for supporting others. I used it everywhere—in business and school especially—to take advantage of people who didn't have the same ability.

I used my memory in school so I could skip classes for weeks, except for the finals' reviews, and I would show up for the tests and pass easily. I used this gift to settle for less than who I could have been, accepting mediocrity as my best.

I Love Me . . .

When the brain tumor and experimental drugs ran their course and my internal memory processing had been disabled to a large degree, I lost the ability to lie—my ability to remember stories I had woven. I had to tell the truth; I couldn't cover for my lies anymore.

For most people, that may seem like a good thing—not being able to lie—but lying was my shield, my steady defense. I had been telling lies to hide actions and beliefs since I was around three years old. I didn't know how to operate without hiding all the bad parts of me. But now I was convinced that if people knew how little I could recall, they would use it against me. It didn't take long to realize that losing my controlled recall stole my ability to protect myself from people who wanted to take advantage.

My education was now lost. My ability to study books and remember dates and facts—gone. My ability to remember things people said, even just a day or week later, was a thing of the past. People would say, "Remember when . . ." and I would nod my head and say yes, but really I couldn't remember any of it. I chose to be a victim of all the negatives this gift being taken from me caused in my life.

It was life, take two! Truth without catches, truth without manipulation, truth without justification. I had to become *real,* really quick! When I get to share a situation or conversation, I have only my truth to depend on. I don't have the ability to keep track of several versions of the event. The season of manipulating one resource to feed or starve another resource was over for me, as the illness that stole my body now had stolen part of my mind as well.

The ability to retain and recall basic information had become unreliable at best, which only created fear of not being able to create or function. I lived in terror that I would be put on the spot and would fail miserably in front of my peers or trainees. I constantly worried about getting asked to write on the flip chart in a seminar. *Everyone will know I can't recall how to spell many words.* I kept a running list that I would use as my spelling guide. I would take it up when I had to write in front of the class, just to make sure I would get the words correct. I had to go through this horrifying process over and over; it was a nightmare that I could not wake up from.

When I was introduced to Klemmer & Associates leadership, I feared this would be just another class I sat in on, but instead Mr. Brian Klemmer told us that motivation and how-tos weren't enough—that we had to experience the "aha." We had to feel it, see it, and own it for ourselves. When we left that three-hour event called a Champion's Workshop, I still had my doubts, yet I could remember each emotional moment. I felt alive again.

That started my journey on retraining my brain to learn, retain, and regurgitate. By the time I had attended Heart of the Samurai, I decided that being a part of Klemmer's mighty lion pride was where I belonged. Yet learning modules, learning energy work, learning the whys behind the whys, wasn't easy. I learned logical and solution thinking. Yes, it took me twice as long as it has taken other facilitators, but I didn't quit. I found something I didn't have to *learn;* it was something I could be.

I made a promise to myself to "be with" like no one before me or since. I knew that I might not remember everything that was said when I was with a student. I couldn't guarantee I could remember every call, statement, or idea, but I could be with people in their pain, in their fog, on their journey. The less I relied on words, the more authentic I became. It wasn't about my talking; it was a new experience of connection with humanity. The less I talked, the more the person in front of me won. I didn't need to be the smartest person in the room; I just had to be willing to hear, willing to be, willing to care. One of the huge results of *being* verses *doing* was the simple blessing produced in my life from simply being quiet.

Because of the lack of control I experienced growing up, I was naturally attracted to a reality that supports reports, agendas, and structure, and I naturally settled into the Advanced Leadership Seminar. I learned my schedule so well that it became auto-thinking, yet I still have moments when I feel like a lost child among familiar symbols and faces.

Fact = Meaning—the Moment of Shift

Rather than seeing my loss of memory and processing disorder as a handicap, I chose to see them as true gifts. For me to retain a memory, the event must have an emotional impact. I need to be emotionally invested in the meaning I create as well or I cannot retain the meaning. This makes fact/meaning much more than a seminar exercise for me; it is crucial to my life's experience, my existence. Once inverted, this meaning becomes my truth.

This gift has helped me make better choices for myself and others. I have to depend on my truth now, not what others say. Sometimes it's awkward. I say what I am thinking, when I am thinking it, no holds barred. I say it because it is my reality in this moment—not to hurt others, but to help them; not to hold back, but to give them even more. My truth isn't what I felt last week; it's today. This moment. Right now.

Many times I have created my own challenges—yes, I have made decisions and taken actions that went against my truth. I am not proud of those moments, but I am an example of someone who seeks growth and development. I can learn from everything, so with time every experience can create a win.

Being the *real* me led to the discovery of the vulnerable me. After all, being open and committed is my only effective and compassionate option now, so I chose to open myself up at a heart level. The who and the what

I discovered inside was pretty special.

So many gifts have come from the experience of the illness and the loss of my memory. The main gift I have gained is intuition. Now, every day, I get to live and love in my daily truth, second by second, moment by moment. I really believe this physical setback was a gift to me. It allowed that old crutch to be stripped from my life. Before, I was so focused on my intellect, my analytical thinking, on my manipulating and moving others for my gain, that I didn't listen to my intuition. Now I lean on it every day.

Are there still times I feel silly because I can't remember a statement I made ten seconds earlier? Of course. Often I can't spell because I can't remember what the word looks like, and I feel foolish. Sometimes in business meetings I simply stay quiet and nod a lot and take notes so I can do the research when I can access the web. In simple moments like those, I still struggle and feel inadequate. I can't remember little things, but these are no longer moments I stay victim to. Now I celebrate the gifts I do have. I celebrate my intuition. There has not been a man, woman, or child I have not connected with intuitively. I get to be connected to God in that moment, and for me, there is simply no greater joy. It is worth everything I have been through and more.

A NOTE TO YOU:

People often ask me about the diagnosis of lupus (and subsequently rheumatoid arthritis) and how I continue the lifestyle I choose to experience. I travel two-thirds of the year come rain, snow, sleet, hail, or heat! I love all aspects of my adventures: flying, new cities and towns, people, seminars, friendships, and giving and receiving a piece of my heart everywhere I go. When you live passionately like I do, you will find and continue to find a way!

I live in physical pain every day, from top to bottom. I listen to professionals and do everything I can do to naturally strengthen my body. I get better and better every day. This may sound courageous or bold or even heroic, and yes there are heroes involved, but that title belongs to my beautiful husband, children, and closest friends. They are the heroes who cover me when I can't get out of bed for a staff meeting after having been awake for forty-eight hours straight. They are the ones who bring me food, medicine, and supplies to make sure I can endure the day.

They are the heroes who remind me that they need something from me instead of resenting me when it is missed; heroes such as Jim Stovall, who coaches me on successful CEO tactics and thought processes; those who invest so much time giving me information, only to remind me a month later as though it were my first time to hear it; those who appreciated all of my gifts and made them special and valuable; those I call my closest friends, who have laughed with me and at me and have believed in me. My loved ones know I have fallen short in both my personal and professional life, yet they have loved me anyway. Because of these heroes, I promise to learn from my mistakes, grow daily as a hungry child does, and be the best version of me I have in this moment.

The reason I tell you all this is to help you understand that fact/meaning isn't always exactly like you imagine it, yet that doesn't indicate that it isn't working. When the mind shifts, the body will follow. Maybe not in my time, yet I will be still and wait.

Nine
DO YOU WANT TO HAVE A LIFE?

TODAY I celebrate all the challenges I have experienced. It is very clear to me that I wouldn't be where I am today if I hadn't been humbled and stretched by the experiences of my past. My heart was broken and healed in specific ways to enable me to help others. I was made to lead others forward in their lives—not because I have something they don't, but because of my desire for everyone to have access to the tools I was given.

My greatest gift from God is the ability to reach into other people's lives and help them pull out the poisonous plants manifesting in their gardens of life. To see people remove and rework their subconscious is awe inspiring. When others replenish, revive, and resurrect their God-given gifts, some from birth and some from wounds, there is nothing else like it. I am forever humbled by those experiences.

I know this to be true because my battle to regain my health led me right to where my gifts were meant to flourish. I've already shared how my mother introduced me to the nutritional supplements that would save my life. As I began to regain my health, I became friends with the woman who sold the products to my family. I will never forget the day I was asked, "Now that you are going to live, do you want to have a life?" (Thank you, Champions. You have blessed hundreds of people, and their lives are forever changed because of your courage to introduce your business and family to Klemmer & Associates through a Champion's Workshop!)

Soon after I was asked that life-changing question, I was personally introduced to one of these three-hour workshops that explain what K&A does. There were about a hundred of us in the room that night, and Brian Klemmer was the presenter. I came from a place of thinking that what he said sounded kind of crazy—kind of out there. I didn't understand a lot of it. There were concepts I had never heard of and I was doubtful. *If this works, why haven't I heard about it before?* I wondered.

But by the end of the night, I thought, *What if this guy is right? What if the stuff he's talking about is true and my life doesn't have to keep looking like this?* It was one small spark, and I made a decision to attend a Personal Mastery Seminar. The rest is pretty much history.

Today I am committed to my health. I have been married for eleven years, and my husband and I live in Durango, Colorado, with our family. I have four well-adjusted, healthy, beautiful, and funny children from the ages of five to twenty-five. I also have two grandbabies. Make no mistake: we are not the poster family for domestic bliss. We are human; we make mistakes. Sometimes the only time we see one another is as we pass in the hallway. Some days we are sad about the time we spend apart, but other days we know it's for the highest good! We come together as a team and from a place of compassion with accountability.

My marriage isn't perfect by any means. We don't expect perfection because it doesn't exist. Our goal is excellence, and we are forgiving of each other when we fall short. We are real humans living real life in real time. We are doing the best we can with what we have, and the tools K&A gave us have allowed us to go from a place of sheer dysfunction to a family working together, striving together, and playing together, one day at a time.

Today I study and work with lessons from the things I've come through. My past shortcomings are always on my radar. Sadly, I don't always catch myself before I cause pain to myself or others. I'm always playing detective and asking questions because life and circumstances keep happening. I have new opportunities, stresses, and mountains to climb, new people in my life, and a higher level of responsibility, so I have to keep a check on myself using coaches, counselors, and friends. I have to ensure I don't stuff my emotions but instead process them in a healthy way.

I work through those things so that I don't revert back to a place where I operate from the stories of *I Love Me Not,* where anxiety, pain, stress, devastation, fear of failure, fear of success, loss, and betrayal are the reality. I am always watching out for the temptation to use an exterior mechanism to numb or distract an inside problem. I realize and encourage the importance of cleaning out and letting go. I acknowledge that relationships and opportunities are more achievable and fulfilling without the internal conflict that taints our view of today.

The same is true in my relationships. I don't care who you are, relationships can be hard. You bring two people together who have different belief systems and life experiences and you hope they will work together in such a way that they have longevity. It's not easy, even in the best circumstances.

One of the biggest lessons I gained from my second marriage is that I taught Eric to treat me the way he did. Because I was brutal to myself internally, on some level I gave him permission to treat me that way. Today I command respect. I give it and I receive it. I am not talking about a military type of deference; it's more of a respect that one loving human being extends to another for no reason other than the fact that both have heartbeats, are experiencing life, and have intrinsic value. I choose to no longer be around people (at least not for long) who aren't considerate, open, and sincere. I eat feedback for breakfast, lunch, and dinner, and I welcome it (that's not to say it's always easy to take), but I no longer accept anybody putting me down, belittling me, or taking from me mentally, emotionally, or spiritually.

Today I stand up for myself. Today I matter. Today I can look in the mirror and recognize that the woman looking back at me is actually worth something. She has done some bad things, she's done some sinful things, yet she's not bad or evil. She makes mistakes, and she's made a lot of them, yet she's not a mistake. She knows she no longer has to allow anyone else's opinion, belief system, or junk to be about her. Nobody can make her feel a certain way unless she allows it, and that is a gift that will continue to give back forever.

Today I like who and what I am becoming. Today I have confidence. I help other men and women in abusive relationships to see the choices they have and the tools available. Through Klemmer & Associates, I have the ability to connect with other people who feel trapped. I have been there.

Because of retraining my brain, through fact/meaning and shifting those belief systems around, I now know that I don't need weight for protection. I have a choice in how I feel and a choice in what I surround myself with. I have a choice in what I do.

I don't need an exterior circumstance to protect me from an interior experience, and I didn't know that before. The more I work with fact/meaning and weight release, the healthier I become. I am becoming stronger. I still work almost every day with the concept of weight release, a healthy diet, and exercise. I am very much focused on the long-term benefits of doing what honors my body now so I can continue this adventure we call life.

I know that if I'm going to travel the world and fulfill my purpose, my physical body needs to be in the best shape possible. Now I see my body as an asset. In the past, it had no value. Instead of using my physical being to hide behind or keep people away, shut people down or suck others in, today I know that my body is a tool. The better I can take care of it, the more I get to live my purpose and the more people I can help.

My relationships with my children are some of the most significant in my life. I came from abuse and neglect, and before I worked for Klemmer & Associates, my older children very much lived that lifestyle. But I am most excited about how my five-year-old and my grandchildren are growing up in a completely different environment. They're held accountable and they're responsible. There's understanding, forgiveness, empowerment, and encouragement—all the things I didn't even realize or understand with my older children.

We are a unit and we travel as a family. We bicker, play, discover, argue, and explore. Those are things I never had with my older children because of my resentment, resistance, and revenge and all the problems I made for myself because of my victim mentality.

I didn't know how to have joy. Today I have joy. I giggle every day. I look forward to going to work, and I look forward to coming home. I would do the work I do for free—and I did for three years. I believed in this work so much that I spent a hundred days out of the year doing K&A seminars, staffing, special projects—volunteering my efforts and not getting paid a dime. It was a clear sign to me that this was my life purpose.

Today my father and I still don't communicate much. But it's not about whether we have a perfect relationship; it's about being at peace. *Am I at peace with how things are?* And today I can say yes.

I have forgiven my father. I have learned to see him as the small child he was: who went through trauma and drama, who was hurt, who was rattled, who wasn't taught. By contrast, my relationship with my father actually highlights the men in my life who have shown up and stood up for me. *Thank you.* Instead of being angry, I use my experience as a tool to energize me to encourage other men to be good daddies. It keeps me focused on the importance of having men come in to model positive male behavior for the teens in our youth program. I am grateful that although I may not have had a daddy like every little girl dreams about, my daughters have one of the world's best daddies in my husband, Tim.

Perhaps the greatest preparation I have experienced has come out of the most difficult challenge in my life: overcoming the sexual abuse and rape. Today I still do the processing work on the psychological aspects of dealing with abuse for that amount of time. That kind of trauma is not something that can be glossed over or casually dismissed. It certainly was not part of God's plan for my life, but it *is* an example of how God works *all* things for our good. It may seem counterintuitive, but out of my greatest pain have come equally powerful lessons.

I now know that you and I can truly have it all! You can be in a relationship and have an emotional connection, a spiritual connection, and a physical connection—not just one but all of them. I never knew that before. Today my relationships are rich and powerful and so deep in a true heart connection that has nothing to do with sex. And it's so much more fulfilling than just the act of sex. Sex is a gift, a coveted experience, a beautiful thing between two people who love each other. Today I get that it is a part *of* love, not love itself.

Each one of these lessons has helped lead me to the place I was created for. My mentor Brian Klemmer suddenly and unexpectedly passed away several years ago from a heart condition. Those of us who knew and loved him were devastated, and there were many challenges that had to be overcome to make his vision a reality. Through the hard work and contributions of countless dedicated people, we are growing and expanding in the United States and around the world, including China, Sweden, Vietnam, Europe, Australia, New Zealand, and the Philippines. K&A is an international organization now, changing lives all across the globe.

What is unique about us is we are an experiential seminar company; we are not a lecture-based seminar company. It's not sit down, watch the PowerPoint presentation, and here are a bunch of how-tos. People actually see, feel, and experience exercises in such a way that they create their revelations; they create their breakthroughs. This takes it from an intellectual understanding to a heart transformation. We do this process in a Compassionate Samurai way, and this is what makes us so successful and unique in the industry, making lasting change for the people who will utilize the tools and the work.

I want to impress upon you that I am not a guru. I don't have all the answers, and I don't think I am better than anyone. The difference between me and you are the tools I was exposed to. And I wasn't just exposed to them; I took them on and still practice them *every day.*

You see, everybody today is reading material, listening to content, hearing about a win-win world, but when push comes to shove, there aren't many people who are putting it into practice. When I get up in the morning, I intend to create a win-win world. Do I always do it? *No.* Do I make mistakes? *Yes.* Have I lied, cheated, and stolen? *Yes.* Even since being in this work? *Yes.* Why? Because belief systems work at the subconscious level, and it takes repetition and emotional involvement to shift them. Sometimes we don't realize what is going on until we see the results—the pain, the disappointment. And what we do in that moment defines our character. Do we own it? Do we apologize? Do we recommit? Do we do the work to repair it? Are we honest with ourselves?

Being happy, healthy, successful, and unified around the world and stopping starvation, sex trafficking, abuse, loss, war, and divorce will take every one of us being the best versions of who we are. The thing is, we have to actually know who we *really are*.

I want to personally challenge you to be the person who wakes up. Don't live as the "walking dead"—dead emotionally and spiritually, not dreaming anymore, not creating abundance, having given up hope, having given up on our fellow man. Be willing to find the greatness within you; find the things that are holding you back from having, being, and doing all you were designed for.

You aren't broken. No matter who you are or where you are in life, there are greater rewards for you, greater accomplishments, deeper connections, deeper love, and stronger faith. We can all do more, we can all be more, and we all have access to infinite possibility. You deserve to wake up in the morning and have joy. You deserve to be able to walk into an environment and not become a victim of the circumstances or people there but instead to shift your environment based on what you want to create.

The reason I chose to share my story is that I want you to understand that in spite of what happens to you, you can overcome. You can experience tragedy and have joy to the same degree. You don't have to be the smartest person, have the most money, or have the easiest life and best opportunities. You can come from nothing and become everything. It takes the willingness to believe something different.

We're all somewhere. Whether it's making a deeper connection or making a million dollars, decide for yourself. What are your desires?

Maybe you want to be a better parent or friend. Maybe you want a more fulfilling spiritual life. Maybe you want to own a business. All of those things are possible because you get to determine your future. No matter what happens, you can have the life you desire if you are willing to do the work. Will it be hard? Yeah, maybe. But I assure you, it is totally worth it.

ABOUT THE AUTHOR

KIMBERLY ZINK is the President/CEO of Klemmer & Associates, The Premiere Leadership and Character Development Company, with offices in both California and Colorado. She and Krystal Zeller came together as business partners to support the 500-year legacy continued by Brian Klemmer, founder of K&A, whose dream was to create an army of Compassionate Samurai to make a difference in this world.

Kimberly holds eight certifications in various coaching disciplines including Executive Coaching, Christian Coaching, Teen Crisis Coaching, Life Coaching, and Life Progress Coaching. As a coach she supports individuals from all walks of life from stay-at-home parents and entrepreneurs to billionaires and CEOs of multinational corporations.

Kimberly recently celebrated her twelfth year as a Senior Facilitator at Klemmer & Associates, having designed and conducted training for over 30,000 students—from all over the world and in several different languages—in Personal Mastery, Advanced Leadership, Heart of the Samurai, and Samurai Camp Seminars. She has also created extraordinary training programs for children and young adults through Klemmer & Associates' Youth Leadership Camps, specializing in training for teens ages 12-18 and Playful Mastery for children ages 5-12.

In addition to coaching and facilitating seminars, Kimberly is a much sought after speaker who is known for inspirational and transformational presentations. In the space of a single presentation, she moves people from average thinking and circumstance-driven living to being fully committed to living victorious lives of their own design and creation.

This is her first of many books to come. Kimberly's message inspires action, not just hope, in those looking to leave the past behind and create a glorious future through the power of choice, no longer living as victims to circumstances. She is renowned for her honest, direct, no-excuses approach as well as her remarkable intuition.

Kimberly resides in Durango Colorado, with her family. She has been married to Tim Zink for 11 years and they have four children: Jonathan, James, Timber, and Lacey (husband Cody). They also have two grandchildren: Syler and Creede. Kimberly is a confident, trusting, peaceful and joyful woman. Her purpose is to communicate with the world heart to heart.

MORE LOVE FOR KIMBERLY ZINK

"Kimberly Zink a powerful, life-changing force. Her love, intuition, steadfastness, and strength of character continue to inspire, motivate, and challenge me and countless others." —Sam Reyes

"Little girls don't know what love is; I can attest to that. Kimberly helped me open the door to my own heart eight years ago, and that experience continues to influence how I love myself."—Lanee Arndt

"Kimberly's message is a very powerful one. Using her own life experiences, she shows us that our past does not define the essence of who we are and that we can make choices every day that move us forward in a positive direction."—Norm Reed

"Kimberly, I learned so much from you and your amazing Klemmer team that I believe saved my marriage and saved me from myself. What I have learned on my Klemmer journey has been tough but has helped me develop into a better person, friend, mentor, coach, wife, and mom. I am grateful every day for investing in myself and my future and taking the leap of faith that led me to you and Klemmer."—Blair Billings, senior national director, BeautiControl

"Kimberly Zink has experienced things that many of us struggle with, yet in her struggles she has found a way to create a positive outcome. She has a way of creating a space where trust and safety are established, allowing others to work through their past and present and into a beautiful future."—Kari Ramon

"When I met Kimberly Zink, I chose to apologize for myself, manipulate others, and believe I would never be enough. Kimberly gently asked me not to apologize for myself and reminded me that I am enough. I have stepped into true leadership and am enjoying the most fulfilling life I can imagine, living in my highest purpose, and loving and laughing with amazing people. I will always love Kimberly for taking a stand for me when I didn't believe in myself."—Joshua Carpenter

"Kimberly, thank you for reminding me that I'm worth it! The practice of self-honoring that I have been doing is one step in a fun, fabulous journey of healing and self-forgiveness."—Sheri Johnson

"Kimberly makes sunshine seem possible for so many people, including me. Thanks, my resilient friend!"—Val Dehline

"Kimberly is a worthy example that we are not defined by our past, whether it be decades ago or yesterday. She reminds me that there is nothing more powerful than a made-up mind. I appreciate her honesty and vulnerability when telling her story and genuinely want to read more about her life experiences."—Traci Oncina

"I believe that Kimberly has the ability to connect with the suffering of others on a heart level and instill hope through her lived experience. She taught me that change is possible once perspective shifts and that my thoughts can be my biggest obstacles. Since learning this, I have started driving again, something that I gave up for eight years because of panic attacks."—Judy Reed

"Kimberly, I want you to know that you are part of my top ten people who have made an impact on my life. You're an incredible human being! My deepest gratitude to you."—Steve Robison

"My two challenges were to pass a CPA exam and get my watercolor paintings in a gallery. I got my master's degree, passed three CPA exams, sold two paintings, and am adding photography to the mix. Kimberly Zink was very instrumental in helping me get here."—Nancy Raybold Staley

"Thank you for all you have added into my life. I'm in a completely different space and enjoying every single moment of my life."—Heather Lambeth

"Kimberly is such an inspiration. I feel so lucky that I was able to spend time with her. I recommend Klemmer & Associates 100 percent. I'm forever changed."—Shelly Dore

"I cannot tell you how magnificent it was seeing Kimberly, sharing her energy and enthusiasm, and feeling so enveloped in her concern and love. I am still walking on cloud nine."—Vicki Barcus

"Kim, you have taught me so much, and I thank you for everything you have done for me as well as so many others!"—Taylor Davidson

"You gave your all and created some real magic! I´m not easily impressed, after having seen so many great speakers, including Brian, but you really blew my mind!"—Eric Thyrell

"Kimberly, thank you for your sacrifice for me and telling me what I needed to hear, not what I wanted to hear. Your heart poured out on me and lifted me from victim to a responsible, Compassionate Samurai who is limitless. I am grateful for you, the other facilitators, and the staff."
—Wesley Murrie

"Kimberly is the most amazing, gifted speaker, coach, and facilitator I have ever experienced in my entire life. Words could not even begin to thank her enough for her huge sacrifice of time and love. I am transformed with a much deeper understanding that I really needed. Kimberly is the most incredible frosting on the perfect cake."—Darlene Nelson

"I adore, respect, and love Kimberly Zink, one of the most courageous women I have been blessed to know. You will not find a more honorable, loving, and committed woman who will go to all lengths to create a world with no one left out."—Autumn DeCosta

"Please know how grateful I am for the work you all do to invest in the lives of people and empower them one by one to never give up. The rippling effect is truly priceless!"—Kathy Hammond

"Having you as a Compassionate Samurai was awesome. I heard from several people that their teen camp experience this summer has been the highlight of their K&A lives to date. I was very touched by what you shared with the camp Saturday. It was intimate and heartfelt, demonstrating a Kimberly some had not known. Thank you for deciding to share more of your life with us during this experience. Know that we are with you in the somber as well as the joyous times of your life. May God's favor enable you to continue your beautiful contribution to the world."—Hank Eichin

"Kimberly, thank you very much for being who you are and all that you bring to our world. You are a very special woman."—Denise Moreland

"Thank you for taking the time to mentor me and guide me in my college journey this last year. It's been my best year by far, and I'm very thankful. Results: I made the Dean's List this quarter with a 3.75 and pushed my overall GPA past a 3.0. I've made a plan to graduate in the next year and a half and have been in a happy relationship for a year now. I'm making small steps, but I'm powering through them. I'm thankful for people like you who believe in me."—Zachary Ludolph

"Kimberly, I'm reading a book that made me think of you and how grateful to God I am for the blessing of you in my life. I realize this is something you probably hear frequently as one who has positively impacted numerous people. However, it is still worthy of saying because I would not be the healthy, courageous, authentic, responsible, trusting woman I am today had I not borne the brunt of your hard, truthful, wonderful chiseling four years ago! Thank you and thank God for your investment of time and tough love!"—Darlene Noe Stetson

"Kimberly Zink is one of the most passionate, intense, and brave people I've ever had the privilege of knowing. Here's to her true beauty!"
—Ada Potata Milby

"You're an amazing trailblazer, Kimberly. My entire family has benefited greatly from knowing you!"—Janine Akins

"Kimberly, you have shown me and others respect in more ways than most people. You have a huge heart. Thank you for all of your amazing support."—Adilyn Kay

"Thank you, KZ! You have helped me change my life in so many ways, and I needed that wake-up call! I can officially say that I am the happiest I have ever been."—Jason N. Mayer

"Kimberly, the knowledge, insight, energy, and love you have was evident in all you shared. I am inspired by you and so grateful that I am now connected to you. Today I had several colleagues approach me to say that they felt there was something different about me. One colleague said I seemed grounded and at peace. Yes, I am."—Shelley Wilson

"I am free of old chains that were trying to choke me and am forever grateful to you. Keep doing what you do. It's quite contagious!"
—Tammy L. Hahn Bond

"Kimberly, I just wanted to encourage you by letting you know how much of an impact camp had on me. I remembered how empowered and accepted I felt, and I continue to use many of the things I learned there. You guys are doing such an amazing job and changing lives. I thank you endlessly!"—Alexa Mbali Keckley

"You are a truly inspirational, courageous, and bold woman who has helped make me an open, caring, vulnerable, connected man!"
—Patrick Ranzieri

"I am a better person because I met you, Coach Kimberly. Thank you for being the amazing and compassionate person you are."—John Bodine

"Dreaming big is what propels us to achieve those dreams. You have helped me realize that, and I'm forever thankful to you for that gift!"
—Teresa Fullan

"You teach us all to dream and that we can have our dreams, whatever they are! Keep teaching us and showing the way!"—Karen Saint

"I remember Kimberly's honest words of encouragement to me and her belief in me. It's great to see her continuing that work. My dreams are coming true one at a time."—Jeff Richcreek

"It takes courage to speak the truth. Thanks for your courage, Kimberly. I'm happy for your success and inspired by your dreams, so keep them coming!"—Brian Inskip

"You are such an amazing role model. So grateful for having you influence my life. My women's program is taking off, and I know it would have been very difficult to achieve without your knowledge of empowering people's lives!"—Julie Balch

"You are an inspiration, and I love you and the work you accomplish. Thank you for all that you have done for me. I have grown so much within the last year and am getting closer to accomplishing my dreams and making every day count."—Rebecca Yates

"Thank you for touching my life. Your fierceness and love hit me like a freight train. I will be forever grateful for the impact you have made in my life. I am blessed."—Jennifer Tardibuaono

"I was so ecstatic to hear of my daughter's positive experience. Her voice was so full of expression and energy, unlike the monotone responses I had received pre-camp! I can't thank you enough for being you and for the love and support you give to these teens. I'm sure this experience has made a huge difference in my daughter's life already."—Teresa Meierhofer

"Thank you from the bottom of my heart for transforming my little girl into someone who says thank you and 'Can I help you with anything?' I love you, woman!"—Elisha Bravo

"I love Kim. If I could choose to be just like someone, it would be her. She is everything I dare to be in life. Kimberly Zink is my hero!"
—Lauren Long

"Kimberly, you are an amazing, powerful, wonderful, loving woman of God. I am very grateful for all that you, your team, and your exceptional staff do for our children. God bless you all."—Tony Buttigieg

"I can't tell you how grateful I am for what you did for me this past week. I will never forget that you changed my life forever."—Christian Bedy

"Kimberly is an amazing woman, and I hold her in incredibly high regard. She stands in her power, loves with her heart, gives unconditionally and with passion, and pushes and challenges people out of their comfort zones for their own benefit. Kim embodies what it is to be a Compassionate Samurai, and I aspire to be as I see her: bold, powerful, successful, loving, kind, generous, committed, passionate, abundant, funny, integral, supportive, and focused."—Fifi Mac

"Before K&A, my life was a mess. My marriage was on the verge of divorce, I hated my job, and I hated myself. My wife, who had filed legal separation papers, had a friend who dragged her to what she assumed was a self-help seminar, her first Personal Master class at K&A. Afterward, she decided to hold off on the separation and take me to my first Personal Mastery class. After talking to her and noticing her changed demeanor, I decided to go, although I was skeptical. That night changed the rest of my life. We took more classes together at K&A, and our relationship has never been better. I love myself, my wife, my kids, and my job!"—Tim Denning

"Kimberly is an angel on earth, a woman of her word, with wisdom, beauty, and boldness."—Cathy Caraway

"The time you invested with Joan and me surrounding our relationship created a major shift and allowed us to move forward. Your insights and energy brought great things for us."—Daniel Ashurst

"I'm a bit hesitant to confer sainthood on Kimberly, as the saint is usually dead when so honored, though I believe in this case we can waive that requirement. To be a saint, one must have challenges along the way. Saints don't sugarcoat the truth. They lovingly strip our falsity and lay us out bare to the world. Saints hold us accountable and beckon us to follow them and reach beyond our shortcomings. This is Kimberly, and we are better for it."—Bruce Carlson

"Kimberly, thank you for being vulnerable and putting it all out there. I will always remember your words when I was up against a wall: 'Stop fighting! Let them help you!' That was when I realized that my hope for the future will come from receiving from others. I am grateful for those words."—Lorry Belhumeur

"You are an inspiring and extremely strong woman. I'm thrilled I got to work with you this past week, and I look forward to doing so again in the future! If you ever need anything, I would be honored to support you, as I know you would do the same for me, and I can't thank you enough for that."—Lauren Kratina

"Kimberly, you and your team are awesome. I look forward to how things will be in our family now that we are all operating from the same place. Thanks for your love and sacrifice."—Hope Walford Ramsay

"Thank you, Kimberly, for shaping the next generation of powerful leaders!"—Bethany Connor

"Kimberly is a bold, trustworthy, and committed professional and leader. She creates results when others just talk and talk some more. She and her group provide an absolutely unique leadership experience with experiential hands-on training that literally pulls owners, executives, managers, and employees together as a unified, powerful team working with purpose. The people they lead will benefit and immediately experience a difference." —Charles N. Vezinaw

"Kimberly is passionate about helping others become the most powerful people possible so they can live their dreams. She is a valuable asset and resource to those she serves and works with. Kimberly is a highly sought-out executive coach and trainer whose clients consistently achieve and exceed their goals. She brings her grounded authenticity to her position and responsibilities and would be a critical asset to any organization."
—John Edwards

"Kimberly is a leader and a great coach. She clearly understands and practices the principles taught at K&A. My experiences with her were all great, and I highly recommend her as a coach, leader, and mentor."
—Flo Lattery

"Kimberly was very easy to work with on several projects requiring many hours. She supported and encouraged me through the whole event. I highly recommend her as a facilitator and to oversee a project to completion."
—Amanda Fillweber

"I have personally been involved in leadership training for more than thirty years and during that time have experienced inspiring and empowering individuals. Kimberly Zink is at the top of that list, as she also brings a compassionate heart that genuinely cares about humanity. She is a master

in assisting others in personal transformation by bringing self-awareness and compassion that will move them forward in a positive direction. She is truly a gift to this world, as she is one of the best in her field."
—Mary Rose Ramirez

"Kimberly is a woman who works with a spirit of excellence and with great personal integrity. I look forward to working with her on many occasions in the future."—Kerry Hitzke

"Kimberly is one of the most powerful and effective coaches I have worked with. As a leadership trainer, she is the best! She has the ability to see us as we really are, not as we are attempting to project. Kimberly's training is a life-changing experience, highly recommended, and worth every penny!"—Eric Anderson

"Kimberly is one of the most incredible, insightful, and effective professional coaches I've encountered in my journey of personal growth. It is a pleasure to watch her in action. I highly recommend her as a coach and trainer."—Karin Pitman

"The word *cannot* is not part of Kimberly's vocabulary. She has a can-do attitude and has done many mission-impossible assignments in all areas of her life. If you are looking for a coach with the highest integrity, Kimberly has my unclouded recommendation."—Peter Geier

"Kimberly is a very detailed facilitator who is highly skilled in communication and coaching. She is results oriented, and that is what makes her such an effective facilitator and coach. She is a person of high integrity. Thanks, Kimberly, for making me who I am today!"
—Daniel Asher

"The world is a better place because of all of you. Thank you for your commitment to K&A."—Katie Bowles

"I am grateful each and every day that I met such a powerful, compassionate, worthy, and confident woman! Kimberly's willingness to share your heart speaks volumes! The mountaintops are so beautiful once we realize they are reachable and available for all!"—Tanya Alexander

"Kimberly's story is one of breakthrough and hope, piercing the heavy darkness of confusion and silence. Her heart to bring change is unlike any other, and I am thankful every day for the quest she has taken up to offer her experience as a light to others who love themselves not."
—Jillian Dillon, Beachbody coach

"Today I am able to be the father I never knew, the husband my wife deserves, and the man God created me to be because I learned so much from Kimberly. No matter how many times I thank her, she gives me the credit for doing the work. Her humble heart is what makes her beauty radiate from the inside out."—Nathan Madrid, US Navy (retired)

"Every now and then, we have the privilege of meeting a person who brings hope and inspiration to others simply by being authentic. Kimberly Zink knows from experience what it is like to hurt to the depth of being and still move on to overcome and bring that ability and vision to others."—Doug Hudson

"I am blessed to have met Kimberly Zink, a wonderful woman who through all of her stuff has the gift to share and teach us how to become more than who we thought we could be. She has taught me what love is

and how to be open and sharing in a way I have never known."
—Patti Bredemeier Marrin, Klemmer Coaching Academy graduate

"Kimberly is a phenomenal facilitator with great insight and an ability to help people see the obstacles in their lives. Kimberly helped me identify choices I was making that were holding me back from reaching my goals and potential. Think big, achieve results, and bring others with you is what Kimberly lives."—Peggy J. Chase, president and CEO, Terros Inc.

"One of the best gifts I ever gave myself was to attend K&A seminars, with Kimberly Zink as my facilitator. It was a life-changing, priceless investment for my life."—Nanci Newhall

"Kimberly Zink touches the lives of many, not just by coaching them to create the lives they desire but by being a living and breathing example of overcoming adversity. Within the K&A framework, Kimberly chose to create a different meaning for her experiences that allowed her to move forward and create a life of love, gratitude, and abundance."
—Janet Evans, family physician and mom

"Kimberly is a beam of light, a ray of sunshine, a pillar of hope, an answer, a new path that impacted more lives than she knows. I've witnessed it, felt it, and now know it. I will forever be thankful for her."—Dani Hoopii, events coordinator, State of Hawaii Organization of Police Officers

"Kimberly is able to put into words what my heart yearns to say. Kimberly is a hero of mine because she not only survives but also thrives."
—Michael F., operations manager

"I met Kimberly Zink at a time in my life when I felt unlovable. Through her acceptance and ability to guide me to connect to others, I now feel full of life, love, and possibility."—Stephen Townsend, materials manager, UnitingCare Health

"As the leader of Klemmer & Associates, Kimberly is able to bless and teach so many thousands with her life lessons of love and compassion. I'm personally so deeply honored to know her and her family, all of whom have the highest intent of doing good in the world. Kimberly is a special blessing to us all."—Reverend Johanna, life coach

"Kimberly Zink is one of the most insightful and intuitive people I have ever known. She and Brian Klemmer have taught me more about how to help people who were traumatized during childhood than I ever learned during five years of formal psychiatric training. I have seen her achieve major healing breakthroughs with students that never occurred for them during years of psychotherapy. She has a God-given gift that continues to help thousands of people."—Timothy G. Roberts, MD, diplomate, American Board of Psychiatry and Neurology

"We all have obstacles in our paths along the way. Many times we cannot see them, but K&A has ways to help us unblock them. This is where Kimberly's story is important in inspiring others to connect with their higher selves and break through any conditions that may have been holding them back. I know her story well because I am privileged and proud to have her call me Dad."—Brian Everhard, real estate investor

"One of the most important moments of my life was meeting Kimberly Zink. When a person oozes that much love, compassion, safety, and truth, it can only mean that she lives what she preaches. In the words of philosopher

Marshall McLuhan, 'The medium is the message.' I believe that nothing describes this woman more: Kimberly Zink is the message."—Benjie Danquah, pastor

"Kimberly Zink went from struggling to survive life's devastating lies as a young girl to become the thriving CEO of Klemmer & Associates, a premier leadership development company that is changing lives all over the world."
—Rick Wonser

"It is hard sometimes to be in control of what happens in our lives, but as a result of our experiences, we can choose to be courageous, compassionate, and wise. The result of such evolution can sometimes leave us breathless. Thank you, Kimberly, for teaching us that one's evolution is limitless!"
—Raluca and Viorel Ciurea, Montreal, Canada

"My dearest friend Kimberly is a strong, passionate, loyal, and full-of-life lady. My daughter is her namesake, as I hoped she would be just as strong, passionate, loyal, and and full of life as Kimberly is."
—Janet Lynn Schmelzer

"I am beyond grateful for Kimberly Zink and the powerful role she has played in my life. Her journey is not only inspiring and encouraging but also a great reminder that all things are possible for those who believe."
—Ronnie Doss

"Kimberly is a fierce, intimidating warrior who uses every ounce of her strength to pull out the light in every one of us. And trust me, she comes out of every encounter scarred, bruised, exhausted—and victorious. I hope every human being has the honor of being in battle with her."
—Nandini Chandarana

"Kimberly Zink is the true essence of love. By choosing new meanings and a desire for truth, she transformed herself into a beautiful butterfly. When she spreads her wings, she creates new life in others!"
—Kimberly V. Flunder

"Kimberly is an exceptional example of a strong, influential, and loving woman. I am a better mom, district attorney, and community leader because I have been coached by her."—Angie Beranek, Rice Lake, Wisconsin

"I love how you controlled the 'facts' and didn't allow them to define or control you. Kimberly, you are so awesome and inspirational!"
—Sheree Fletcher

"I am a better mom, wife, and friend as a direct result of Kimberly's teaching others how to be willing to truly see themselves. My entire family has been enriched because of what she has given me."—Lisa Asbill

"Kimberly's input into my life and so many of my children's and grandchildren's lives is incalculable. She is a spiritual, insightful, courageous, and vulnerable woman. Her sacrifice and gifts are immeasurable."—Stephanie K. Schneider

"If it hadn't been for Kimberly's willingness to share her past experiences, I am not sure I would have trusted anyone enough to start removing the bricks from the walls of my past and allow others in. I am still a work in progress, but Kimberly has given me the hope and inspiration to keep going."—Candy Carpenter

"Kimberly Zink's story of being raped, lost, unworthy, and broken resonated with me at a heart level. My life has forever been changed since the day I met her, and I am grateful for her vulnerability and tenacity to overcome her obstacles and share her heart with the world."
—Chelsea Rathie

"Kimberly Zink reminds me that anything is possible if one sets clear intention and no matter what, never ever gives up."—Ernest Furtado

"I believe that one of the primary principles of success in life is to make friends with at least one overcomer. Kimberly continues to create huge results despite horrific events in her past. Her future is bright."
—D. Scott Pullan

"I would not be the woman I am today had I not met Kimberly and come to understand all I was capable of creating in my life. She is an example of a friend, leader, and truly Compassionate Samurai."—Carla Palazzolo, certified life coach

"Kimberly instilled in me that everything is a choice. We get to choose how we feel about things and how we react to them, as well as what we choose to carry as baggage. All of those little things that suck energy, like being cut off in traffic or arguments that are seriously insignificant, just don't even matte. I love what this woman brings to the world!"
—Trish TrickiT

"Something I learned from Kimberly is 'soft eyes.' I had no idea that when I was concentrating, it made me look mad. I think my wrinkles are actually fading now."—Neitha Wilkey

"On a plane flight back home from a K&A Advanced Leadership graduation, I told my mom that I would somehow return to my last company, where I had been mistreated, in the capacity as a consultant, training the staff who once scarred me so deeply, to heal them (and myself) while creating value for them personally and professionally. I felt it in my heart but did not know how it would come about. Tonight that vision manifested, and I will be facing my fears and overcoming them in three days. Mind-set and communication training starts Tuesday! Kimberly Zink, this is only one layer of how you've touched my life!"
—ShariSodetani KaseyLe

"Kimberly encouraged me to keep moving forward no matter how painful. There was nothing holding me back except me!"—Joanne Rando-Moon

"I was sexually abused as an infant, and although I have no memory of that time, it did affect my life. I had trust issues with others as well as difficulty with intimacy in relationships. I avoided taking time to connect with people at a heart level. I also saw myself as unworthy of accomplishing great things and was afraid of taking risks. Hearing Kimberly's story and how she walked through her pain and into her greatness showed me that I could step into my greatness too."
—Pauline Pawlik

"Change? Transformation is more like it. My family and I no longer take a victim viewpoint. We choose greatness and look for win-win scenarios every day. Thanks, Kimberly, for working so hard with us and never giving up in your life or ours."—The Graf family

"I had no idea this lovely woman of God would soon change my life. Kimberly helped me learn that crying is okay and is a form of healing.

She also taught me how to make heart-wrenching choices on my own and to always show my inspiring smile. I live by the motto 'Every moment is a choice, and every choice has prices and benefits.' Thank you, Kimberly, for never stopping believing in me."—Katelyn Holmstrom

"All of us have our burdens to bear; no one is exempt. If Kimberly can overcome the trials that were given her to become one of the most powerful, influential, and healing women I have ever known, what then could possibly stand in the way of my achieving my own dreams? Nothing whatsoever. Kimberly is a stupendous model of the power of intention, and I am honored to call her a friend and mentor."—Chris DeSantis

"Kimberly's story challenges all my excuses—for hiding, for pretending, for not wanting more. She calls me out and calls me to action. Let's stop the pretending and instead stand proud as the real, gutsy, broken, victorious, growing, and limitless people we are. From the bottom of my heart, I thank her for leading the way."—Susan Stevenson

PRAISE FOR KLEMMER & ASSOCIATES

"Klemmer has changed my life. Thanks for all you do!"—Rebeca Vasquez Bermudez

"I'm a better man because of this work and will be a better husband and father. That kind of growth is invaluable, especially when creating a new pattern of family unlike the one I was raised in."—Auren O'Connell

"Much love to the staff, students, and facilitators of K&A. I'm so honored to be a part of Brian Klemmer's five-hundred-year plan." —Hannah Thomas

"Thank you for making teen camp a transformative experience for both of my sons. I am so excited to hear about their experiences and am really amazed at what they got out of it. They sound so grounded and wise for their age."—Marianna Dobrovolny

"I am so grateful to Scott, Kimberly, and the rest of the team for the amazing work they have done. I sent my daughter and got back a dynamic, amazing warrior."—Tom Akins

"K&A has been a life-changing experience for me. I plan to work with them as long as I can, and I want my friends to learn what I have learned at this camp. Thank you so much for everything you have done!" —Ben Paris

"Thank you for allowing my three kids to be a part of your wonderful camp. One of my goals was to have them come together even closer as siblings, and I can see that already happening."—Sherry Ward

KIMBERLY'S BABY PHOTO

MATERNITY HOME IN *Louisiana*, WHEN MY MOM DROPPED ME OFF.

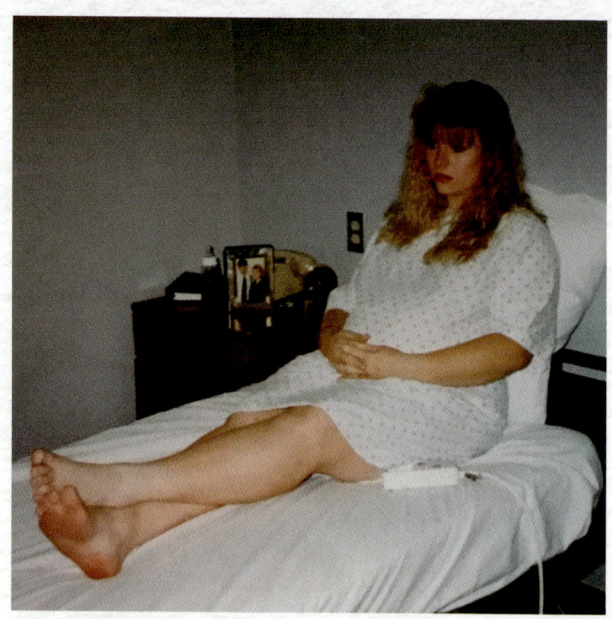

Kimberly, AGE 19, HAVING *Lacey* ALONE AT THE HOSPITAL WHILE HUSBAND IS AWAY AT BOOT CAMP.

Kimberly, Jonathon, Lacey, and James, 1999

Zach, Lacey, Jonathon, Courtney, James, and Samantha

Kimberly Zink, overweight

Kimberly Zink and friend

Kimberly Zink, 2003

Kimberly with team of networkers.

Tim & Kimberly Zink, 2005

Tim & Kimberly Zink

Krystal Zellmer, Kimmichelle Pullan, Kimberly Zink, and Pam Cross, Klemmer & Associates Executive Team

Krystal Zellmer & Tim Zink at Heart of the Samurai, San Diego

Timber Zink

Tim, Timber, & Kimberly Zink
at Preschool Graduation.

Kimberly and Timber Zink at Three Springs.

Kimberly & Timber Zink at Contribution Project.

Timber Zink at Heart of the Samurai.

Tim. & Timber Zink for Daddy-Daughter Dance.

The boys and their princess Timber.

Jonathon Brady Thompson raising funds for the homeless "his way!"

Tim & Kimberly Zink, Durango, Colorado

Krystal & Henry Zellmer at Ropes Course, Colorado

Cody and Lacey Johnston with grandchildren Syler and Creede, Colorado

James Zink & nephew Creede Timothy Johnston

The Zink Family being "Our Own Kind of Crazy"

The Zink Family, 2016
We aren't perfect, yet we are perfect for us!